METHODS IN
THE STUDY OF
HUMAN BEHAVIOR

METHODS IN THE STUDY OF HUMAN BEHAVIOR

VERNON ELLINGSTAD
NORMAN W. HEIMSTRA

The University of South Dakota

BROOKS/COLE PUBLISHING COMPANY
MONTEREY, CALIFORNIA
A DIVISION OF WADSWORTH PUBLISHING COMPANY, INC.

ISBN: 0-8185-0131-6
L.C. Catalog Card No.: 74-79470
Printed in the United States of America
10 9 8 7 6 5 4 3 2 1

Manuscript Editor: Grace Holloway
Production Editor: Meredith Mullins
Illustrations: Creative Repro, Monterey, California
Typesetting: Holmes Composition Service, San Jose, California
Printing & Binding: Malloy Lithographing, Inc., Ann Arbor, Michigan

PREFACE

This book provides an overview of behavioral research methods and is designed as a supplement for any introductory course in education or the behavioral sciences. It includes the topics of traditional concern, such as measurement, selection and assignment of subjects, and methods of observing behavior, as well as several topics of contemporary interest, such as research ethics (particularly the problem of the deception of human subjects), the publication of research findings, the applicability of research findings to practical problems, and the problem of obtaining funds for research.

Any book reflects the author's biases about what is appropriate material and about how the material should be presented. We have used frequent examples because we feel they are an effective way to facilitate an understanding of the principles discussed. We also feel that students do not have to be exposed to statistics in detail in order to understand research methods. Consequently, in the body of the text, we have dealt with statistics at a conceptual level rather than a mathematical level. However, the statistical appendix at the end of the book includes some of the basic mathematical developments of these statistical procedures.

A number of people contributed in many ways to this book. We wish to thank reviewers Marilynn B. Brewer at the University of California, Santa Barbara, David W. Martin at New Mexico State University, Roger E. Kirk at Baylor University, and Daniel Lordahl at Florida State University for their comments on the manuscript. We also wish to express our appreciation to several people at Brooks/Cole Publishing Company who provided us with valuable assistance at all stages in the development of the book: Bill Hicks, Grace Holloway, Bernard Dix, and Meredith Mullins. To the students in our undergraduate courses who helped us formulate the final version we owe a particular debt of gratitude. Finally, we wish to express our appreciation to Mrs. Susie Radigan for her skillful and patient typing of the manuscript.

Vernon S. Ellingstad
Norman W. Heimstra

v

CONTENTS

METHODS IN THE STUDY OF HUMAN BEHAVIOR

INTRODUCTION

As B. F. Skinner (1953) has noted:

> Behavior is a difficult subject matter, not because it is inaccessible, but because it is extremely complex. Since it is a process, rather than a thing, it cannot be easily held for observation. It is changing, fluid, and evanescent, and for this reason it makes great technical demands upon the ingenuity and energy of the scientist [p. 15].

This book is about the methods used to study behavior. It will become apparent in this text that the study of behavior does indeed make demands on the ingenuity of the researcher; and we will spend considerable time describing how these demands have been met.

Why is behavior difficult to study? Behavior is something we all engage in, we can observe it, and we all know a great deal about it. Thus, we can often predict fairly accurately what people we know reasonably well will do under certain circumstances. Studying behavior at this casual level is not particularly difficult. At this level, however, many of our observations of behavior are incorrect, and our ideas about the behavior of people in general do not hold up under careful analysis. It is when we attempt to study behavior scientifically that the difficulty of the subject matter becomes apparent.

SCIENTIFIC RESEARCH

Research in the behavioral sciences—or, for that matter, in any of the sciences—can be thought of as a process designed to find answers to questions by means of scientific techniques. We will consider these techniques in detail. However, scientific research also depends on the research attitude of the investigator applying the techniques. For a proper research attitude, "every statement, every principle, every pronouncement by oneself or by another should be examined from two points of view: whether or not it is true and, even more important, how one could go about assessing its truth or falsity" (Scott & Wertheimer, 1962, p. 9).

The first point in this definition emphasizes that the researcher should be concerned with facts rather than with what he or others have said about the facts. Many researchers have difficulty developing this attitude because it involves the rejection of authority and the recognition of the fallibility of existing knowledge. The researcher must also be able to accept facts when they contradict what he wishes were true. The second point in the definition, how one could go about assessing the truth or falsity of a "fact," involves understanding research techniques.

The kinds of questions that a researcher attempts to answer are, of course, quite diverse and depend upon many factors. Some questions are generated by practical problems arising from the technological nature of our society, from the behavior of individuals in our society, and from other "real world" sources. For example, what is the most efficient design, from the driver's point of view, of an automobile's dashboard? What effect does long exposure to loud noises have on an individual's behavior? What aspect of a driver's behavior is most likely to lead to an accident? How can we modify attitudes toward minority groups? Such questions give rise to problem-solving research, directed at a practical, applied goal.

Much research, however, is aimed at answering not specific practical questions but questions that either help develop a theory or test a theory already in existence. Typically, in theory-developing research the questions that the researcher attempts to answer are not very precise; they may be asked in the form of "What do you suppose would happen if I were to ...?" or "What might be the effects of variable X on behavior Z?" For example, an investigator may wonder what effect a certain type of noise will have on people's ability to learn to perform a particular task. He does not know whether the noise will facilitate learning, inhibit learning, or have no effect, and he performs an experiment to find out.

In theory-testing research the questions are typically more specific. Suppose that two theories have been advanced on the effects of noise on behavior. One theory predicts that high intensity noise will make the individual work faster at a particular task; the other theory predicts that he will work slower. In this case a study can be designed to answer the question "Does high intensity noise make a person work faster or slower?"

We could spend much more time talking about research and about what we mean by the research process, but doing so would quickly involve us in a more detailed discussion of the philosophy of science and of the scientific method than is warranted. Consequently, we will reiterate that research is the process designed to find answers to questions by means of scientific procedures and leave it at that.

Motivations for Doing Research

As pointed out, some research is conducted merely to satisfy the curiosity of the investigator, while other research is aimed at solving a pressing real world problem. Obviously, there are many types of studies that fall between these two extremes. Regardless of the type of research that an investigator pursues, however, at some stage in his career he has asked himself, "Why do research?"

One of the primary reasons that many investigators do research is that it is for them a highly pleasurable activity. Scott and Wertheimer (1962) state:

> Perhaps what motivates most investigators is that using one's creative and intellectual powers to add something novel—something nobody else ever knew before—to the storehouse of human knowledge is an enormously rich and satisfying experience. Not that the average researcher is likely during his career to make a world-shaking discovery; a great deal of enjoyment can still be derived from the process of following an idea wherever it leads. Doing a difficult creative job well, according to one's own high standards, provides one of the greatest satisfactions that can be experienced, a depth of pleasure that can hardly be matched by anything else [p. 3].

Many other factors may, of course, motivate an individual to engage in research. For example, a number of scientists are hired by laboratories or other institutions to work on research projects. Whether they derive a great deal of satisfaction from conducting research under these circumstances will depend on the individuals involved. In the scientific community the research that a person conducts (frequently the amount, not the quality) determines his status and is used as a criterion for raises, promotions, and so forth. In academic settings, where the "publish or perish" attitude often prevails, the motivation for research may be simply to hold on to one's job. Some investigators may do research to support a theory in which they strongly believe, while other researchers may be motivated to work just as hard to disprove the theory.

WHAT IS BEHAVIOR?

We have noted that behavior is difficult to study scientifically. As used by behavioral scientists, the term "behavior" encompasses an extremely wide range of activities—probably much wider than the typical reader would consider to be "behavior." When a psychologist refers to the behavior of an organism, he is referring to any form of activity on the part of the organism that is observable either directly or with the aid of instruments. Observing some forms of behavior may require elaborate instruments, as in the case of studying electrical changes in the brain, or special tests to ascertain, for example, certain mental characteristics. Still other kinds of behavior can be easily seen—the investigator may simply observe the behavior of interest and jot down his observations on a notepad. The point to keep in mind is that behavior ranges from very subtle activities, such as brain waves, to activities that are readily observable. One has only to scan the *Psychological Abstracts*, which present nonevaluative summaries of the studies in psychology and related disciplines, to obtain an idea of the variety of types of behavior studied. In reading only a few of the 20,000 or so studies abstracted annually, one cannot help being impressed with the diverse activities of humans and other animals that behavioral scientists select for study.

As will become apparent, the selection of the particular kind of behavior to be observed is a critical consideration in any investigation. Although the objectives of the study will determine to a great extent the behavior selected for observation, a number of factors must be taken into account in the selection process. The methods employed by the investigator in conducting his research will be determined largely by the kind or kinds of behavior to be observed. The behavior involved will also help to determine the manner in which the researcher organizes and examines his observations and the statistical tools he uses in his examination. We will deal in more detail later with the factors to be considered in the selection of the behavior to observe.

THE RESEARCH PROCESS

The research process consists of a number of steps or stages. Though all research projects will differ to some extent, so that listing a series of stages that would accurately define all types of investigations is not feasible, certain procedures are common to nearly all studies. An initial step in any investigation is the formulation and statement of the research problem—that is, getting an idea about a particular area of interest and then stating the idea in a researchable form. This stage is often preceded or followed by an extensive review of the scientific literature in the area. Thus, a literature review can be considered to be another important step in the research process. Designing and conducting the investigation are two more steps; they are followed by analyzing the data and, finally, writing the report. Much of this text is concerned with these last four stages.

In this section we will deal briefly with the stages of formulating and stating the research problem and reviewing the literature. We will consider in some detail, however, a stage in the research process that is extremely critical and that is often ignored in textbooks on research methods. This is the stage in which the investigator attempts to obtain funding for his research project. No matter how important the problem the researcher is interested in and how sophisticated his research design, he cannot conduct his research if he cannot obtain funding. Some investigators would like to remain aloof from this aspect of research, but the realities of life make it impossible to do so.

Formulation and Statement of the Research Problem

At one time or another, when learning of a scientific breakthrough or an interesting research project, the reader may have asked himself, "I wonder how the researcher got the idea for that study?" Many people in the scientific fields have asked themselves the same question and have conducted studies of "creativity" among scientists. Although an essential first step in any research project is an idea that can be stated in a researchable form, just how an investigator develops an idea for a research project is not easily described or, for that matter, completely understood. Typically, a scientist develops an idea for a research project as a result of being so familiar with a particular field that gaps in the existing knowledge about the field are apparent to him. In some instances, however, brilliant projects are developed by individuals who are relatively new to a given field. Whether a research idea usually develops through a formal deductive process or through some kind of intuitive process is speculative. Regardless of the manner in which the research idea developed, it is a necessary first step in a research project.

We cannot assume that as soon as the researcher has an idea he can design an investigation based on it, for the idea may be only a rather general and, perhaps, even confused notion. An adequate statement of the research problem requires that the investigator formulate his idea clearly and completely. Doing so may take some time and involve considerable review of the research literature in the area and, sometimes, research of an exploratory nature. Once the idea is formulated, the investigator can usually state the research problem clearly and unambiguously in question form. This transformation of an often vague initial idea into a precise statement of a research problem, or question, that is amenable to scientific research is critical if the research is to produce meaningful information. Numerous articles have been written on the criteria for good research problem statements, but, basically, if the question derived from the initial idea has been stated in a form that can be empirically tested or answered, the problem statement will usually be satisfactory.

That the question asked must be amenable to testing may seem obvious. However, many interesting questions are asked that cannot be tested or, at best, are extremely difficult to test, sometimes because of the nature of the subject matter. Many philosophic and theological questions are of this type. An extreme example is the question that concerned many medieval theologians about how many angels can dance on the head of a pin. Often the question asked in the problem statement, although dealing with a researchable area, is so broad that it is impossible to design a study that will answer the question as stated. In this case the researcher has the choice of dropping the idea completely or narrowing it down to such an extent that it becomes feasible to investigate. The mark of a good researcher, then, is the ability not only to generate good research ideas but also to transform these ideas into problem statements that can be subjected to scientific research.

Reviewing the Professional Literature in the Field

As we have pointed out, if an investigator is to conduct research in a particular scientific field, he must understand the previous research performed by others. Typically, an investigator keeps up with the research in his field by reading selected journals as they are published, attending professional meetings, and corresponding with other researchers working in the same field. When the researcher is attempting to design a study in a field in which he has worked for years, he is often completely familiar with previous research and does very little in the way of a literature review.

In many instances, however, the research idea may involve the investigator in areas of which he does not have a thorough knowledge. In these cases he must review the relevant literature to become familiar with any previous studies that are similar to what he has in mind. Sometimes he will find that another researcher has already done a study that has answered the question; sometimes he will find very little in the literature that is of help in developing his research idea. At any rate, knowledge of what others have done in the field will prevent an investigator from duplicating previous research and, when his idea is original, will help to clarify it and to enable him to state it in a researchable form. Reviewing the literature will also give the researcher valuable notions about experimental designs and techniques employed by other investigators that may be useful in designing his own studies.

We will not attempt here a detailed discussion of the many approaches to reviewing the literature in a particular field. Briefly, a researcher in the behavioral sciences, particularly psychology, typically begins his review by carefully searching the *Psychological Abstracts*, published by the American Psychological Association. These contain brief accounts of articles published in nearly all the world's journals of interest to psychologists. Each issue of the *Abstracts* contains both a subject and an author index, and the *Abstracts* are cross-indexed in several ways. An annual subject and author index is also published. Thus, an investigator can search the annual index for references that seem relevant to his research idea, read the abstracts in the various issues to determine whether they are indeed of interest, and then go to the original articles for detailed study. The *Psychological Abstracts*, available in virtually every library at colleges and universities with psychology departments, are probably the most useful tools for a literature review in the behavioral sciences.

Also available are several abstract journals that are restricted to more specific areas than are the *Psychological Abstracts*. If a researcher plans to work in one of these areas, he would typically use one of these more specialized journals. For example, an investigator interested in human factors in man-machine systems or in the effects of various aspects of the physical environment on performance would consult the *Ergonomics Abstracts*. Other specialized abstract journals concentrate on areas ranging from child behavior to psychopharmacology.

Of particular value to an investigator attempting to review the literature in a particular field are articles that summarize the research in the area. The *Annual Review of Psychology* includes chapters on most of the major areas of psychology that stress the recent research in each area. An *Annual Review* is also published each year in a variety of other scientific disciplines. The *Psychological Bulletin*, a journal published by the American Psychological Association, also contains reviews of literature in various areas of psychology.

There are, of course, many other sources to which an investigator can go to bring himself up to date in a particular area. Various organizations with computerized retrieval systems will (usually for a fee) supply an investigator with references or abstracts. Sometimes a researcher will hire a graduate student to conduct the initial review. But regardless of how the investigator goes about reviewing the available literature in a field, it is a critical stage of the research process.

Funding the Research

The stage of funding the research usually occurs between the design stage and the phase when the study is actually conducted. Investigations involving only a pencil, a notepad, and the experimenter's time are rare. Usually, even investigations that appear to be relatively simple cost a surprising amount of money. Consequently, even though many investigators would prefer not to be bothered with such mundane matters, if they are going to do research they will have to find some source of financial support.

The behavioral scientist's research is sometimes supported by funds from his own institution or organization. Thus, colleges and universities often have a research fund for financing projects by faculty members. (We might mention, however, that in these days of tight university budgets, the research funds are generally the first to go.) Sometimes the investigator pays for his research out of his own pocket. Typically, however he seeks support from some agency or organization whose prime function, or at least one of its functions, is to support research. A surprising number of organizations help finance research. Virtually every branch of the federal government offers substantial amounts of money to support research in the behavioral sciences. Indeed, the primary function of several agencies, such as the National Science Foundation and various divisions of the U. S. Public Health Service, is the support of research, much of it in the behavioral sciences. Each of the branches of the military spends a great deal of money on behavioral research, as do a large number of private foundations and other groups. A few moments spent browsing through the *Annual Register of Grant Support* (Academic Media, Orange, N. J.), a comprehensive source of information on existing forms of financial aid for researchers, cannot help impressing the reader regarding the wide variety of support channels available to behavioral scientists.

If there are so many sources of support, why is there any problem obtaining funds to conduct research? The answer is simple. The amount of money requested annually by researchers far exceeds the total amount of money available from the various funding agencies. Consequently, obtaining research funds becomes a very competitive situation and requires considerable time and effort on the part of the researcher. Although there are various ways of applying for and receiving funds from granting agencies, in almost all cases some form of research proposal is required. Such proposals may differ widely, but most have some features in common in both the content of the proposal and the manner in which it is reviewed by the agency.

Preparing the Research Proposal.   Most proposals fall into one of two categories: the *solicited* proposal and the *unsolicited* proposal. As the name implies, a solicited proposal is one prepared in response to a request from some granting agency. For example, a government agency may want to know what effects fatigue may have on driving performance. The agency prepares a Request for Proposal (RFP) outlining in some detail the type of project wanted. The agency then distributes copies of this RFP to a number of investigators and laboratories. An investigator who receives an RFP may or may not prepare a proposal in response. The proposals received are then evaluated by a group of experts, and the investigator or organization that submitted the best proposal is awarded a research contract. An unsolicited proposal, on the other hand, is based on a question of the investigator that he wishes to answer by means of a research project. He prepares the research proposal and submits it to a granting agency. In other words, the proposal is unsolicited by the agency.

Regardless of whether the proposals are solicited or unsolicited, they all have certain characteristics in common and follow a more or less standard format. As an example, let us consider the format for proposals submitted to the U.S. Public Health Service.

On the first few pages of the proposal, the applicant completes items requesting data about the institution, the total cost of the project, a broad statement of objectives, biographical sketches of the professional personnel who will be involved in the project, and a detailed budget estimate. The investigator then completes the "research plan" portion of the proposal, which, from the reviewers' standpoint, is the most important section. The U.S. Public Health Service suggests that the outline given below be followed in preparing the proposal. This outline is taken directly from U.S. Public Health Service Form 398 (Information and Instructions for Application for Research Grant).

A. Introduction:
   1. Objective: State the overall objective or long-term goal of the proposed research.
   2. Background: Review the most significant previous work and describe the current status of research, including your own, in this field. Document with references. In a new application, describe any preliminary work you have done which led to this proposal.
   3. Rationale: Present concisely the rationale behind your approach to the problem.
B. Specific Aims: List your specific objectives for the total period of requested support.
C. Methods of Procedure: Give details of your research plan, including a description of the experiments or other work you propose to do; the methods, species of animals, and techniques you plan to use; the kinds of data you expect to obtain; and the means by which you plan to analyze or interpret the data to attain your objectives. Include if appropriate a discussion of pitfalls you might encounter, and of the limitations of the procedures you propose to use.

   Insofar as you can, describe the principal experiments or observations in the sequence in which you plan to carry them out and indicate, if possible, a tentative schedule of the main steps of the investigation within the project period requested.
D. Significance: What is the potential importance of the proposed work? Discuss any novel ideas or contributions which your project offers. Make clear the health-related implications of your research.
E. Facilities Available: Describe the facilities available to you for this project, including laboratories, clinical resources, office space, animal quarters, etc. List major items of equipment available for this work.

Depending on the type of proposal, the above outline may be modified somewhat, and additional information may be included. If the outline is carefully followed, the reviewers of the proposal will have all the information they require to judge the merit of the proposal.

Note that a detailed budget estimate is required as part of the proposal. The budget, of course, will depend on the type of project that the investigator has in mind or that has been requested by an RFP. The U.S. Public Health Service proposal suggests that the applicant's budget request be broken down into categories, such as personnel, consultant costs, equipment, supplies, travel, alterations and renovations, and "other expenses," which includes the cost of publishing the results of the research, communications costs, and so forth. These are called the *direct costs* of a research project.

Nearly all granting agencies also include *indirect costs* as part of the total amount granted. The reason for paying the indirect costs is to reimburse the university or other organization where the research takes place for the costs incurred in supporting the research. These costs may include the cost of heat, lights, office space, additional personnel in the accounting office to handle the grant funds, and so forth. Thus, a researcher may ask for $50,000 to support a project (direct costs), but paying the indirect costs as well may bring the grant to $75,000.

Review of the Research Proposal. The exact method of reviewing a proposal differs according to the agency from which funds have been requested. Typically, however, the review involves several steps. Most agencies have review panels made up of experts from within the agency or of outside experts from universities, laboratories, industry, and so on. The members of these panels have a chance to study carefully the proposals assigned to them and then meet to discuss the proposals and to assign a ranking to each one. The reviewers consider a number of factors in deciding on the merit of a particular proposal. They not only consider very carefully the research plan but also consider the research background and experience of the investigator, the facilities available for the project, and the amount of money the applicant has requested. Thus, the final ranking that a proposal receives may be dependent on a number of factors. It may be approved with a high or low ranking, or it may be rejected.

Before the final ranking the reviewers often decide that they would like to talk to the investigator personally and to visit the laboratory where he proposes to do the research. In these cases a site visit is scheduled, and several members of the review group visit the investigator. This is a useful procedure for clearing up questions about the research plan and giving the reviewers a better basis for making their decisions.

Even if the review panel has been favorably impressed with a research proposal and has given it a high ranking, the applicant is by no means assured that his project will be funded. In most granting agencies, after the review panels have met and evaluated the proposals, another decision must be made about the funding because the amount of money required to fund all the approved proposals usually far exceeds the amount actually available. Thus, even though a proposal may have considerable merit and may be approved by the review panel, it may not be funded. The fortunate investigator will receive a letter beginning with a statement to the effect that "Your research proposal has been approved and funded"; the unlucky investigator will receive one stating, "Although your research proposal has been approved, we regret that due to limited funds . . . . "

We have emphasized in this section the steps required of an investigator who hopes to fund a research project. Our reason for doing so is that, as Krathwohl (1966) notes, most people envision

> the researcher as one who dreams up creative ideas, the needed resources miraculously appear, and the hero, in a state of eager anticipation, begins his investigation. Those of us who are researchers would add some less romantic steps, one of which, the preparation of the proposal to make the resources "miraculously appear," has become quite important [p. 3].

Other Stages in the Research Process

We have discussed the problem formulation and statement stage of the research process, the literature review stage, and the problems associated with the funding stage. The design of the study, the actual conducting of the study, the analysis of the data, and the writing of the report on the research findings have been mentioned only in passing. Each of these stages is critical to the research process and will be discussed in detail in the following chapters.

SOME RESEARCH ISSUES

As we shall see later, there are a number of controversial issues concerning the specific methods employed in the study of behavior. Many of these issues are narrow ones restricted to arguments about the superiority of one method or statistical tool over another. However, some issues are broader ones that most behavioral scientists consider to be important. We cannot discuss all of these, but at this point we will consider two issues that seem particularly important: the issue of basic versus applied research and the issue of ethics in research involving human subjects. Other issues will be considered later at various points in the text.

Basic versus Applied Research

In recent years an increasing number of researchers have been designing and conducting experiments aimed at solving real world problems—problems that range from those threatening to disrupt or even destroy society to those inconveniencing some members of society. An example of the former is the problem of overpopulation, while an example of the latter is a piece of machinery that presents its operator with some difficulties because certain psychological considerations were omitted in its design. All kinds of other real world problems exist between these two extremes. Studies dealing with these kinds of problems are called *applied* research and are in contrast to the majority of investigations conducted that have no obvious relationship to the types of problems we encounter in everyday life.

Many behavioral scientists feel that their research should be directed toward increasing our fund of general knowledge about behavior. These investigators are not concerned about whether the information gathered in their research can be used to solve any of the practical, real world problems that man encounters. This type of research is often labeled *basic* or *pure* research.

Although some behavioral scientists strongly advocate one type of research or the other as the only appropriate kind, researchers are increasingly realizing that both types are necessary if the behavioral sciences are to advance. Thus, many scientists feel that the distinction made between basic research and applied research is spurious. These investigators argue that real world problems often arise because of deficiencies in our store of basic knowledge and that research designed to solve practical problems may remedy these deficiencies.

One can cite many examples of research prompted by practical problems that has contributed significantly to the basic literature; conversely, one can also find many examples of basic research that has proved to be extremely helpful in solving practical problems. The field of programed and computer-aided instruction, for instance, which the reader may already have encountered in his education, developed largely from the basic research on operant conditioning conducted by B. F. Skinner. On the other hand, a good deal of what we know about the fundamental processes involved in attention is the result of Donald Broadbent's work, which was originally motivated by practical problems encountered by British seamen on aircraft carriers. Though his research was generated by a military need, it has helped to answer questions about attention that are of great theoretical interest.

The point to keep in mind is that although many researchers are engaged in applied research aimed at solving some of our pressing real world problems, much of this research is possible only because of the foundation of knowledge laid by basic research conducted over the years. However, much of applied research also contributes to this basic fund of knowledge about human behavior.

Some investigators argue that qualitative differences often exist between basic and applied research. These investigators feel that in many cases basic research is neater and follows more closely the principles of good experimental design than does applied research. We have already stated, however, that research is a process designed to find answers to questions by means of scientific procedures. Research is good to the extent that it answers the question and to the extent that confidence can be placed in the answer. Thus, when a basic research program answers the question that was of concern, it is good research, just as applied research is when it answers a question. From this point of view, the difference between basic and applied research is obviously not in the methods employed or in the neatness of the experimental design but in the nature of the questions that the researchers attempt to answer.

The Ethics of Research

Certain ethical considerations are shared by investigators in all scientific disciplines. For example, it is assumed that all researchers are careful in collecting their data and that no investigator would consider falsifying his data. Similarly, it is assumed that a researcher will give credit to other individuals involved in the research by naming them co-authors in the report of the study or in some other appropriate fashion. There are also less obvious ethical considerations concerning the analysis of the data (which will be discussed later) and the publication of the research findings. In the latter case questions arise about publishing the same findings more than once, premature publication of findings, and withholding findings from publication.

We have already mentioned that much research is designed to solve real world problems. In many instances the research is conducted for the military, and the problems being solved may be strictly military. Some researchers refuse to conduct these types of studies on what they consider to be ethical grounds. However, this is a matter of personal opinion. Though one researcher may feel that it is unethical to work on these types of projects, another may consider it not only ethical but his patriotic duty.

The above ethical issues are of concern to behavioral scientists as well as scientists in many other disciplines, and we could profitably discuss them in considerably more detail. However, in this section we will be concerned with some of the ethical considerations particularly important to researchers studying human behavior.

The Use and Misuse of Human Subjects.   As we have indicated, the behavior that researchers study encompasses a wide range of activities, and observing these activities involves a number of different strategies. In many studies, especially laboratory studies, the person being observed knows that he is a subject for an investigation, and his role in the study may be reasonably clear to him. However, in other types of investigations, the individual being observed may not even be aware that he is a subject or, if he is aware, may have been led to believe that the purpose of the study is different from what it is. The way in which subjects are obtained for a study and the way in which they are used during the study have become major issues in behavioral research.

The manner in which subjects are selected for an investigation involves ethical considerations as well as methodological considerations, which will be discussed in detail later. One of the most important ethical questions a researcher must consider in obtaining human subjects for his experiment has to do with the subjects' freedom of choice to participate in the experiment. Coercive measures are often used to obtain the coopera- tion of subjects in research projects. For example, students in introduc- tory psychology classes (one of the most common sources of subjects) must frequently participate in various experiments to meet the course requirement. Similarly, employees in business and industry are often required to take part in studies, as are military personnel. Although the American Psychological Association has established guidelines on coer- cion of subjects, the extent to which it is ethically acceptable to coerce a person to take part in a study is still a question that each researcher must resolve for himself.

Closely related to the problem of subject coercion is that of obtaining informed consent from a subject. Basically, "informed con- sent" means that a subject's decision to take part in an investigation is made on the basis of adequate and accurate information about what he will be called upon to do in the study. Ethical problems arise here because many studies cannot be conducted if the subject is informed about all the details of the study. Thus, potential subjects may often be deceived to obtain their agreement to participate. As we shall soon see, this deception may continue throughout the investigation.

The design of a particular study may require that a subject be exposed to electric shock; to high levels of noise; to vibration, heat, or cold; or to other noxious physical stimuli. As one might assume, a responsible investigator takes great care to ensure that his subjects are not exposed to a situation that will cause any type of permanent damage. The federal government requires that studies involving drugs, for example, be supervised by a physician. Safeguards are also built into the research process to prevent physical damage to human subjects. For example, the government agencies that supply the funds for most research require that each proposed research project involving human subjects be screened by a "human subjects" committee at the institution where the proposal originated. Consequently, even if an investigator proposed a study that might harm the subjects involved, it is unlikely that it would get by the screening committee. There is little chance, then, that a subject in a study will actually be harmed in any physical way. The ethical considerations here are quite clear: An investigator does not conduct studies that will physically harm a subject.

Another matter altogether is the possible damage to a subject in studies in which he has been deceived in one way or another. Most investigations conducted by behavioral scientists require that the subjects be deceived, at least to a certain extent. The degree of deception may vary considerably, but the fact remains that deception often does take place. Some examples of behavioral research will illustrate the kinds of deception used.

Case 1.1. In a study of the effects of motivation on performance, the investigator was interested in comparing the performance on a psychomotor task of groups of subjects who thought they were going to be operating the device for varying periods. Actually, he was interested only in performance during the first 20 minutes. The subjects in one group were told that they would be operating the device for one hour, while those in another group were told that they would be involved for five hours. However, after the 20-minute period each subject, regardless of the group to which he had been assigned, was released and told that the equipment had failed.

Case 1.2. In a study on motivation and performance, freshmen were asked to perform a psychomotor task. Shortly after each subject had begun the task, he was informed that his performance was not at the level of a group of sophomores previously tested. No sophomores had been used in the study; the subjects were told this to increase their motivation.

Case 1.3. An army radio operator, on what he considered to be a routine training exercise, suddenly heard an explosion outside his tent. An officer ran in and told him that several soldiers had been wounded by a grenade accident and to radio for help. The operator found that his radio would not work and was told to fix it as quickly as possible. He did not know that no one had been hurt and that he was a subject in a study of performance under stress. The researcher was interested in how quickly the operator could repair his radio.

Case 1.4. In a study concerned with the effects of aggression on various kinds of behavior, the investigator developed aggression in some of his subjects by giving them a written test and then loudly berating them, in front of others, for their poor performance on the test even though they might have done well.

Case 1.5. A group of people were brought together in a room for a stated purpose and were unaware that they were subjects in an experiment. Suddenly shouts and cries for help came from an adjacent room. The investigator in this case was studying bystander intervention and was interested in whether any of the subjects would go into the next room to help the person in distress and, if they did, how long it took them to decide to do so.

Case 1.6. A group of subjects in a study were given a test, and half of the subjects were told that, on the basis of the test results, they appeared to have homicidal tendencies. The test revealed nothing of the sort. The investigator was interested in determining the effects of this false information on performance on additional tests.

We could cite numerous other studies in which deception of one sort or another was used. Indeed, a significant number of the investigations reported in the psychological literature involve deception of some kind.

Some Views on Deception. Kelman (1967, p. 4), in an article entitled "Human Use of Human Subjects," asks an interesting question that illustrates the entire problem of the ethics of deception. He wonders whether researchers have the right to risk adding to the many anxieties that already exist in life purely for the purpose of experimentation. From the above examples it should be obvious that subjects may be exposed to severe mental stress as part of an experiment. Even if the subjects are carefully debriefed after the investigation is completed (and often this is not done), the long-term effects of some kinds of deception can only be guessed at. However, even when long-term harmful effects are not likely to occur, other considerations are involved, as Kelman points out:

> Serious ethical issues are raised by deception per se and the kind of use of human beings that it implies. In our other interhuman relationships, most of us would never think of doing the kinds of things that we do to our subjects—exposing others to lies and tricks, deliberately misleading them about the purposes of the interaction or withholding pertinent information, making promises or giving assurances that we intend to disregard. We would view such behavior as a violation of the respect to which all fellow humans are entitled and of the whole basis of our relationship with them. Yet we seem to forget that the experimenter-subject relationship—whatever else it is—is a *real* interhuman relationship, in which we have responsibility toward the subject as another human being whose dignity we must preserve [p. 5].

The problem of deception of subjects, then, is a serious one that all investigators must consider carefully in designing their studies. Because of the nature of behavioral research, much of it could not be conducted if deception of some type were not involved. Thus, the researcher might have to ask himself whether the study is important enough to warrant using the kind of deception it would involve. If he decides that the study is important enough, he should certainly be as careful as possible to reduce the mental stress involved and to make sure that all the subjects understand the nature of the deception after the study is completed.

Methodological Implications of Deception. Since this book is about the methods used in behavioral research, the methodological implications of deception should also be taken into consideration although the ethical aspects seem to stir more controversy. Deception is used in research because it is assumed that valid conclusions could not be drawn if the subjects were aware of certain conditions of the study. We further assume that the subjects are unaware that they are being deceived; if this were not so, the purpose of using deception would be defeated. However, this assumption presents a problem. It is becoming more and more difficult to find naïve subjects for psychological experiments, particularly among college students. Although the subjects may be uncertain of what the experiment is about, they generally assume that it is not what the experimenter says it is. The subjects' suspicion that they are being deceived in some fashion may affect the results of the study. Thus, although it may be necessary to use deception in some types of studies, the psychologist who undertakes a study with the assumption that he has naïve subjects is actually being naïve himself.

Another Ethical Consideration

We have discussed in some detail the problems associated with obtaining human subjects for research and the treatment of these subjects during the course of an experiment. A great deal of behavioral research, however, is conducted with subhuman animal subjects, and ethical considerations are also involved in the use of these kinds of subjects.

The American Psychological Association has prepared for its members guidelines on the care and use of animals in research. Similar guidelines have been issued by other organizations and the federal government. These guidelines differ in specific requirements, but all are designed to ensure humane treatment of animals used in research projects. Although space does not permit a detailed discussion of what is considered proper treatment of animals, several of the more important aspects of the care and use of laboratory animals will be briefly noted.

Nearly all guidelines on the use of animals in research have specific recommendations concerning the housing of laboratory animals. Obviously, the requirements would differ somewhat depending on the type of animal used, but any housing system should be designed with the animals' physical comfort in mind. Physical comfort involves such factors as keeping the animals clean and dry, maintaining adequate temperature control, assuring freedom of movement, granting access to food and water, and so forth. The guidelines recognize that a particular investigation may require modification of some of these factors, so that the professional judgment of the investigator will be involved in determining just what modifications should be made.

In many studies animals are exposed to pain, whether after surgery or as part of the experimental treatment. Again, although there are specific guidelines on animal surgery, postsurgical care, and the use of painful experimental treatment, the experimenter is still required to make his own decision about the treatment the animals will receive as part of his experiment. When the treatment will be painful, the researcher must ask himself whether the experiment is important enough to justify such treatment.

The guidelines also deal with how animals should be disposed of after the completion of a study. The choice of a method will depend on whether postmortem tests are to be performed on the animals, since some methods will modify tissues and cause other changes that would make postmortem tests misleading. However, regardless of which of the many available methods is employed, the killing of the animals must be humane.

At one time, because some researchers were negligent in their care and use of laboratory animals, many people were opposed to the use of animals as research subjects. Although on rare occasions an investigator might still be subject to criticism, there are enough laws and regulations on proper animal care that a researcher who continued to use animals improperly would soon be out of business.

SUMMARY

Research in psychology and other sciences is a process designed to find answers to questions by means of scientific procedures. Some questions are generated by practical, real-world problems and give rise to problem-solving research. Other questions give rise to theory development and theory-testing research.

The reasons for conducting research are complex. Many investigators do research because they find it a very satisfying experience. However, research is often conducted because it is expected of a scientist and because salary increases, promotions, and so forth depend on number of publications.

The research process consists of a number of steps or stages. Although research projects differ and will involve different stages, most include the formulation and statement of the problem, review of the scientific literature in the area, design and execution of the study, data analysis, and report writing. Another important stage in any research project is obtaining the funding to conduct the project. This stage typically involves preparing a detailed research proposal and submitting it to appropriate funding agencies for review.

A number of issues and controversies revolve around scientific research. One issue is the question of basic versus applied research, with some investigators arguing for basic research and others for applied research. However, both kinds of research are essential. There are also ethical considerations in research, particularly when human subjects are involved. Guidelines are available for investigators to use in taking care that no physical or psychological damage results from an experiment. Similarly, researchers working with nonhuman subjects must take steps to ensure their well-being.

RESEARCH VARIABLES AND MEASUREMENT

2

The primary purpose of behavioral research is to evaluate cause and effect relationships involving behavioral processes. No matter what research strategy we employ, we seek to describe and explain the effects of independent variables (characteristics of the research subject or his environmental situation) on a dependent variable (a particular aspect of the subject's behavior). The psychologist who conducts a study to compare the running speed of thirsty versus nonthirsty rats in a maze, for example, has defined the research question he seeks to answer by selecting degree of thirst (or perhaps the length of time the rats have been deprived of water) as the independent variable and running speed as the dependent variable. His investigation might then be considered a test of the presence of a cause and effect relationship between thirst and running speed. Similarly, the sociologist who compares the responses of urban and rural residents to a questionnaire measuring the need for privacy is attempting to determine the influence of the independent variable (residence) on the dependent variable (need for privacy).

This chapter is about the way in which the behavioral scientist chooses the appropriate variables and the way in which these variables can be quantified to permit the analysis of his research results.

SELECTING THE DEPENDENT VARIABLE

More than any other single decision made by the researcher, the choice of a dependent variable is the key to the quality and usefulness of his investigation. Unfortunately, many behavioral scientists have overlooked the importance of this step to their investigations and have not adequately defined the dependent variables to be measured. The reader will be cautioned repeatedly in this text to avoid selecting a dependent variable simply because it is convenient and easy to measure. This point cannot, however, be overstated. The choice of a dependent variable essentially defines the research question whose answer is sought in a study. If we choose poorly, we will automatically distort the research question and invalidate the outcome of the project.

To illustrate the importance of careful selection of a dependent variable, let us consider a somewhat extreme hypothetical research situation.

Case 2.1. A physician decided to conduct a study designed to assess the effects of a new tranquilizer on the anxiety of some of his patients. To do so, he selected a group of anxious individuals and measured the length of their fingernails, administered the drug, and then a week later again measured their fingernail length. His assumption in selecting fingernail length as the dependent variable was that fingernail chewing is a frequently exhibited characteristic of anxious persons, so that the amount of anxiety would be reflected by the length of the subjects' fingernails. The physician found no difference in the mean fingernail length of his subjects between the two test sessions (separated by one week) and concluded that the new drug is not an effective anxiety-reducing agent.

Although this example is extreme, it serves to illustrate that the answer to a research question is determined by the experimenter's choice of a dependent variable. First, we note that the dependent variable (fingernail length) is linked to the phenomenon of interest (anxiety) only by assumption or hypothesis. A series of inferences are suggested by the choice of fingernail length as a measure of anxiety. The physician is suggesting, first, that anxiety, which can be considered a nonobservable internal process, is reflected in the overt behavior of fingernail chewing. Second, he suggests that this overt behavior will produce a measurable change in the physical attribute of fingernail length.

The second assumption is not particularly difficult to accept. It seems quite logical to assume that, if one chews one's fingernails, the length of the nails will be affected and that the length of the nails will indeed be measurable, although we might be somewhat cautious in assuming that fingernails will grow fast enough in one week to be measurably longer even if the subject does not continue to chew them. The first assumption, however, raises some questions. Anxiety is, of course, a complex psychological process that can be expected to manifest itself in a multitude of different ways. The investigator in this example arbitrarily selected an extremely simplistic index of this condition. A very real danger in this approach is to pick a measure that does not universally represent the overt manifestation of anxiety. Some anxious individuals, for example, might never consider biting their fingernails but might instead beat their wives. A better measure in these cases might be the number of bruises on various parts of their wives' anatomy.

These points are related, of course, to considerations of the validity of the dependent variable, a topic we will consider in some detail later in this chapter. To avoid these difficulties in the selection of the dependent variable, it is very important that the investigator be well versed in the processes he intends to study. Thorough study of other research conducted in the area of interest and careful, critical planning are perhaps the surest ways to avoid errors at this stage of the research process.

SELECTING THE INDEPENDENT VARIABLES

Although the researcher must assure himself that his dependent variable really represents the process, or behavior, he wishes to measure, it is equally important that he give careful attention to his selection of the independent variable or variables. Here again, variables of convenience are all too commonly chosen, and the quality of the research suffers as a result. The independent variable in behavioral research can be one of two basic types. One type of independent variable is a classificatory variable, representing some characteristic of the research subject. This type of independent variable is extremely common in sociological research but is widely used in other behavioral sciences as well. Consider the following examples:

Case 2.2. A sociological study compares the number of children in families from different socioeconomic classes as defined by the income of the head of the household.

Case 2.3. A comparative psychologist interested in evolutionary differences in animal intelligence conducts an investigation comparing the performance of rhesus, pigtail, and squirrel monkeys on a discrimination learning problem.

Case 2.4. A study is conducted comparing the frequency of occurrence of emotional disorders as a function of the type of child-rearing procedures practiced in the home.

In each of these cases, the independent variable selected represents some relatively fixed characteristic of the research subjects, and the research process involves an examination of the effects of this variable on the dependent variable of interest or an examination of the relationship between the independent and the dependent variable.

The other type of independent variable is a particular aspect of the research situation in which the dependent variable is measured. The use of such environmental or situational independent variables is also common in virtually all forms of behavioral research.

Case 2.5. A study in educational methods compares the performance of children of similar intelligence and ability as a function of different teaching methods.

Case 2.6. An environmental psychologist interested in the effects of noise on human performance compares the tracking performance of two groups of similar subjects under different levels of background noise.

Case 2.7. The psychologist concerned with the influence of thirst on the running speed of rats compares the average running speed of two groups of rats. One of the groups is tested after 12 hours of water deprivation, while the other group is tested after having had an abundant supply of water available in their cages.

In contrast to cases 2.2, 2.3, and 2.4, these examples all involve the use of independent variables concerned with the treatment of the research subjects rather than characteristics of the subjects themselves. In research with these situational or environmental types of independent variables, care is ordinarily taken, in fact, to eliminate differences in subject characteristics between treatment groups or conditions.

As we have indicated, selecting the appropriate type of independent variable is extremely important to the quality of a particular research project. Another important consideration in the specification of the independent variable is the levels of the independent variable chosen for a particular investigation. In a study concerned with the effects of age on attitudes toward sexual permissiveness, for example, it would be important to specify very carefully just what age groups will be compared. Entirely different results could be expected if, for instance, one investigation used 10-to-20-year-olds as a young group and 20-to-30-year-olds as an old group, while another study defined its young group as individuals 10-30 years old and its old group as subjects over 60 years of age. Although the independent variable (age) is the same in both of these examples, the levels of the independent variable are different, and these differences can be expected to alter the research question to which the study is addressed.

Similarly, in investigations using situational or treatment conditions as the independent variable, it is important to consider not only the type but also the levels of the independent variable. In a study of the effects of noise on tracking performance, for instance, we must define exactly what we mean by a "noise condition" and a "quiet condition" if these are the specified levels of the independent variable, noise. We might define our quiet condition as a situation in which the level of background acoustic energy (noise) is 50 decibels. Obviously, 50 db is not really quiet, since in absolute terms quiet is a total absence of acoustic stimulation. Under normal circumstances, however, people are constantly exposed to acoustic stimuli, and 50 db is probably no more intense an exposure than we would encounter sitting at home in our relatively quiet living room. The noise condition of our investigation must also be empirically defined as a particular sound pressure level. Once again, different results can be expected depending on the particular levels of the independent variable selected for the study.

Although no universal rule of thumb applies to the selection of independent variables and the specification of the levels of these variables to be used in a given study, the researcher usually employs a number of strategies. First, in making both decisions, he must consider the research objectives on which his study is based. Second, a review of the scientific literature in the field will ordinarily assist him in his choices. And finally, he may decide to conduct a *pilot* study prior to his actual research project to define more clearly the type and levels of the independent variable that will best answer his research question. This pilot study might be a small-scale version of the actual research project, perhaps with fewer research subjects. Thus, the sociologist conducting research on the effects of socioeconomic status on attitudes toward welfare programs might decide to conduct a small-scale study before implementing a full-scale research project. The results of the pilot survey might help to clarify the definition of socioeconomic status as an independent variable and to guide the researcher in the selection of the appropriate levels of this variable for his full-scale study. It should be noted, of course, that pilot studies are just as useful in the evaluation of the dependent variables. By conducting a pilot study, our sociologist might be able not only to refine his selection of levels of the independent variable (socioeconomic status) but also to evaluate the adequacy of his measure of attitudes toward welfare programs.

MEASUREMENT OF BEHAVIOR

Up to this point we have been concerned with the problems that the behavioral scientist confronts in deciding what behavior to observe and measure (selecting the dependent variable) and under what circumstances to measure the behavior (selecting the independent variable). We will now turn our attention to the measurement process itself and explore various techniques of quantifying observations of behavior.

Scales of Measurement

Measurement in any science is the process of quantifying observations. In the behavioral sciences this process consists of assigning numbers or other labels to the behavior under investigation. Measurement is the basis for all scientific undertakings. Only when our observations of behavior are quantified according to generally accepted or at least generally understood rules is it possible to verify hypotheses about behavioral processes or to assess the influence of independent variables on dependent variables.

Because the range of behavior that behavioral scientists may legitimately study is so broad, they use a number of different types of measurement. Each type of measurement is distinguished by a set of rules dictating how numbers are assigned to observations. These different sets of rules, or scales of measurement, in turn determine the amount of information gained by applying the measurement to the behavior in question. There are four basic scales of measurement for the quantification of observations. We will discuss each of these in turn.

The Nominal Scale. The simplest type of measurement is obtained with the nominal scale. The only rule for the assignment of numbers (or other meaningful labels) to observations under this scale of measurement is the determination of the equality of observations. If two observations are the same on the attribute being measured, they are given the same number or label; if they are different, they are given different labels. Some common examples of nominal scales with which we have all had experience are sex, race, religious preference, political affiliation, and hair color. In each case individuals are placed in one or another mutually exclusive category and labeled with respect to a particular attribute. The only information gained from nominal measurement is the determination of the category into which each observation falls and the relative or absolute number of observations falling into each category. The only statistical operation permissible with the nominal scale of measurement is the process of counting—that is, tallying the number of observations in each category. The process of counting does, however, provide the researcher with a way to summarize observations of behavior made on the nominal scale.

Frequency Distributions. One means of summarizing large amounts of data to permit their interpretation involves the simple graphic presentation of the data in the form of a frequency distribution. Consider the following hypothetical research project, which would yield nominal scale measurement of the dependent variable:

Case 2.8. A comparative psychologist conducted a study on the activity patterns of juvenile and adult baboons in their natural environment. He compiled a detailed list of all the kinds of behavior that the baboons might engage in (reviewing previous research and conducting a pilot study might have assisted him in this process). The psychologist then observed selected juvenile and adult baboons at five-second intervals and recorded which of the categories of activity the animal was engaged in at that moment. Five adult and five juvenile baboons were observed for a five-minute period, resulting in 60 separate recorded observations per animal, or 300 observations of the juveniles and 300 of the adults.

Having expended considerable energy in the collection of these nominal scale data, our comparative psychologist now needs something more helpful than a list of 600 nominal observations of baboon activity on which to base his comparison of the two groups. To describe the behavior of the animals, he might decide to depict graphically the *frequencies* with which each type of behavior occurred in the two groups in the *histogram*, or bar graph, shown in Figure 2.1.

The *abscissa*, or horizontal axis, of this figure shows the different categories of behavior; the *ordinate*, or vertical axis, is the frequency count, or number of times each kind of behavior occurred. A solid bar is drawn above each class of behavior for the young and adult baboons. The

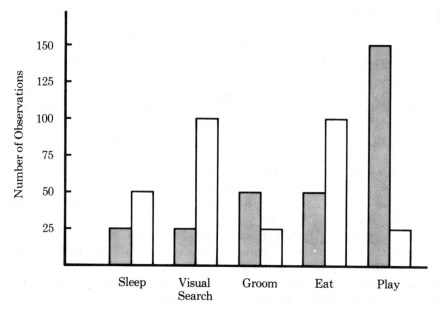

FIGURE 2.1.   A histogram, or bar graph. The filled columns represent the behavior of young baboons and the open columns the behavior of adults.

height of each bar represents the number of times that this activity was observed in each group.

The *frequency polygon* shown in Figure 2.2 presents the same information in a different form. In this case each point on the graph represents the number of times that a particular behavior was observed in a given group of animals. The points for each group are connected to form a continuous line, with the filled circles representing the juvenile baboons and the open circles the adults.

Although the histogram and the frequency polygon provide us with a useful means of summarizing sets of nominal scale data, it is also useful to be able to characterize our data with a single statistical index. The *mode* is such a *descriptive statistic*. It represents our best guess on the measurement class most representative of a particular frequency distribution. (Additional detail on descriptive and inferential statistical methods can be found in the Appendix.) Very simply, the mode is the most frequently occurring category or measurement class. In our example the *modal*, or most frequently occurring, behavior in the young animals is play; for the adult baboons the frequency distribution is characterized by two modes, since both visual search and eating were

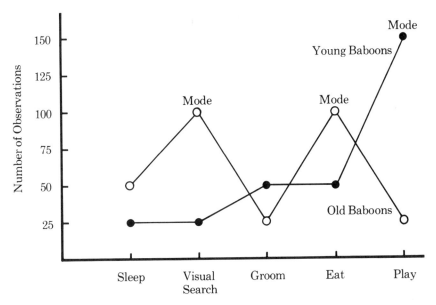

FIGURE 2.2.   Frequency polygon showing the same data as
Figure 2.1.

observed to occur an equal number of times. Thus, the frequency
distribution for the adult animals is *bimodal*, or characterized by more
than one average response category.

The Ordinal Scale.   A different and somewhat more exacting set
of measurement rules gives rise to a second scale of measurement—the
ordinal scale. Ordinal measurement requires that observations be able to
be ordered, or ranked, according to the degree to which they reflect the
attribute being measured. Determining the equality of observations
(classification) is still a characteristic of ordinal measurement, but to this
process is added the ranking operation. A simple and familiar example of
ordinal measurement is class rank. We can distinguish among freshman,
sophomore, junior, and senior students and assign the appropriate label to
each student in a given sample. This process is not simple nominal
measurement, however, since a fixed and constant order is implied by this
measurement of class standing. The category "freshman" always implies
a lower class rank than "sophomore," which is in turn a lesser rank than
"junior," and all these categories rank below "senior." We might point
out here that the choice of category labels is not particularly significant in
either the nominal or the ordinal scale of measurement. We can use either

numbers or verbal labels as long as the basic rules by which these labels are assigned are followed. In fact, nominal scale labels are frequently more descriptive of the categories. We do find numeric labels more frequently associated with ordinal measurement, however, because it is often more convenient to indicate rank with numbers.

It should be apparent that measurement on the ordinal scale gives us substantially more information about the phenomenon under investigation than does nominal measurement. The ordinal scale adds an indication of rank or amount to the determination of equality characteristic of the nominal scale. Thus, in our example of class rank, we know not only that a sophomore is different from a freshman but also that he possesses more of this attribute (class rank).

Another very common example of ordinal measurement is encountered in the assessment of attitude in such questionnaire items as the one below. The respondent is asked to express his attitude toward the U.N. by selecting one of five ranked categories. If one respondent checks category 4 (effective) and another respondent checks category 2 (ineffective), we know that our two subjects' attitudes toward the U.N. are different and also that the attitude of the first subject is more positive than that of the second. We cannot, however, assess the size of the difference in attitude between the two subjects. Suppose that a third respondent checks category 5 (very effective). We now know that subject 1 has a more positive attitude than subject 2 and that subject 3 has a more positive attitude than subject 1. But we cannot assume that the difference between the attitudes of subjects 1 and 3 is of the same magnitude as the difference between subjects 1 and 2. We know only that subject 3 expressed the most positive attitude, that subject 1 ranked second, and that subject 2 ranked last.

"Which of the following describes your attitude toward the United Nations?"

Very Ineffective	Ineffective	No Opinion	Effective	Very Effective
1	2	3	4	5

Describing Ordinal Scale Distributions.   If our measurement of the dependent variable satisfies the requirements of the ordinal scale of measurement, we can use, in addition to the descriptive methods discussed in connection with nominal scale data, slightly more elaborate descriptive statistics. These statistics convey more information about the distribution of measures. The most useful descriptive statistic in ordinal scale measurement is the *median* (midpoint) of a particular set of scores.

Suppose, for example, that we asked our "attitude toward the U.N." question of ten individuals and obtained the responses shown in Table 2.1. In this example three individuals have indicated that the U.N. is very effective, two that it is effective, two that it is ineffective, and three that it is very ineffective. None of the individuals used the "no opinion" category. The median, or midpoint of this distribution of scores, is one half of the difference between the response of individual 5 and the response of individual 6; for exactly one half of the subjects in this sample had a higher score, while one half obtained a lower score. Category 3 is therefore at the exact center of this distribution of scores. The median tells us that the group attitude toward the U.N. is neutral because of the even split between pro and con. To calculate the median of any set of scores, the researcher merely orders the scores from highest to lowest and then determines the point at which 50 percent of the scores are higher and 50 percent lower. It should again be emphasized, however, that our measures must possess at least ordinal scale properties for the median to be a meaningful measure. Additional detail on this and other statistical measures can be found in the Appendix.

The Interval Scale.   A more rigorous type of measurement is made possible by expanding the set of rules governing the assignment of numbers on the ordinal scale to include the stipulation that the intervals between numeric designations be of equal size. Thus, in interval scale

TABLE 2.1.   Hypothetical responses of ten individuals to the question "Which of the following describes your attitude toward the United Nations?"

Very Ineffective 1	Ineffective 2	No Opinion 3	Effective 4	Very Effective 5

Individual	*Category Checked*	
1	5	
2	5	
3	5	
4	4	
5	4	
		(Midpoint)
6	2	
7	2	
8	1	
9	1	
10	1	

measures the difference between the quantities represented by a 1 and a 4 is implied to be the same as the difference between those represented by a 4 and a 7. In interval measures three units separate each pair of observations, so we are able to make statements about the relative amounts of the attribute measured.

The common household thermometer is an example of an instrument with an interval scale. Most of these devices register temperature in degrees Fahrenheit, the others in degrees Centigrade. In either case the degree lines on the thermometer are an equal distance apart, and the difference between 40° and 50° is equivalent to the difference between 90° and 100°. The origin of the Fahrenheit scale is, however, an arbitrary zero point and does not reflect an absolute zero, or the absence of temperature. This is the case with all measures having interval scale properties; the origin is arbitrarily assigned and does not reflect the absence of the quality being measured.

An interval measure frequently encountered in behavioral research involves the assessment of intelligence. Although there is some controversy over whether IQ tests really represent interval rather than ordinal scale measurement, we will assume for the purpose of illustration that IQ tests do satisfy the interval scale rules. In this case the reference point of a scale of intelligence is usually defined as an IQ of 100, which is assumed to be the average intelligence quotient of the population. Here again, the difference between IQs of 90 and 100 is assumed to be equal to the difference between IQs of 115 and 125. Since the scale is not anchored to a zero point reflecting the absence of intelligence, however, we cannot form ratios of two observations. It is meaningless, for example, to suggest that an individual with an IQ of 180 is twice as intelligent as another individual with an IQ of 90. We can say only that both observations are equidistant from an IQ of 135.

Measurement on the interval scale does, however, provide a great deal more information than do measures possessing only ordinal or nominal scale characteristics. This type of measurement is also amenable to a variety of statistical manipulations not permitted with nominal and ordinal measures

The Arithmetic Mean.   Because of its more sophisticated measurement properties, the interval scale permits much more mathematical manipulation of the numbers assigned to observations than do the nominal and ordinal scales. A descriptive statistic particularly useful in interval scale measurement is the *mean*, or average of a distribution of scores. The mean is obtained by adding the set of observations and dividing by the number of observations. Thus, if we administer an IQ test to ten individuals, we can compute the mean IQ of the group by adding the ten

IQ scores together and dividing by ten (the number of subjects tested). Provided that our measurement of the dependent variable does in fact represent interval scale measurement, the mean provides a more informative description of the average performance of the group than would the median, or mode, which of course can also be computed with interval scale data.

Naturally, it is possible to compute the mean of a set of ordinal or even nominal data if each category on the scale is represented by a number. It is difficult, however, to interpret the mean of a distribution of ordinal data because the intervals between the numeric category designations are not equal.

The Ratio Scale. A still more rigorous type of measurement useful for many attributes comes through application of the ratio scale. In addition to the features characteristic of interval scale measures, the ratio scale rules require the measurement of an attribute to be in reference to a rational zero point representing the absence of that attribute. The most common ratio scales are found in connection with the physical measurement of the attributes of objects, such as length and weight. In the behavioral sciences time-related attributes of various types of behavior are frequently measured on a ratio scale. Reaction time, the time required to respond to the onset of a stimulus, represents such a scale. The measurement of reaction time is referenced to a zero point, or the absence of a time differential between stimulus and response. With this type of measurement, we can construct meaningful ratios of two measurements; we can say, for example, that an individual with a reaction time of one second responded twice as fast as a subject with a two-second reaction time.

Most behavioral scientists would prefer their measurement of behavior to possess ratio scale characteristics, since this type of measurement is by far the most precise. Unfortunately, in many if not most situations, this precise a measurement of behavior is not possible, so we must be content to use scales of measurement quantifying behavior according to less rigorous rules.

Instruments of Measurement

Having selected his dependent and independent variables and having determined exactly what he will seek to measure and what kind of measurement will be made, the researcher must now consider what tools he will use to accomplish the measurement and to record his observations. This process of implementing the measurement of behavior may be very simple or extremely complex depending on the nature of the dependent variable and the conditions of the specific study.

To some extent the complexity of the measurement process depends on the scale of measurement used. Thus, nominal scale data ordinarily require less sophisticated measuring instruments than do interval or ratio scale measurements. Our comparative psychologist studying baboon behavior might, for example, use the simple measuring instrument depicted in Figure 2.3. This instrument is nothing more than a tally sheet on which the psychologist records the number of times a given animal engaged in each of the five types of behavior. At the end of the observation period, the researcher simply counts the number of marks in each column. For this particular investigation, this simple measurement and recording device may be entirely satisfactory.

Animal No. *3*		Group *Juvenile*		
Date *1/17/74*		Time *2 PM*		
Sleep	Visual Search	Groom	Eat	Play
////	卌 //	卌 卌 //	卌 卌 //	卌 卌 卌 卌 卌

FIGURE 2.3. A tally sheet for recording behavioral observations. Each mark represents a single nominal scale classification of the behavior of the animal being observed.

Questionnaires and interview protocols are another relatively simple and straightforward measurement tool frequently used in behavioral research. A portion of an actual questionnaire is reproduced in Figure 2.4 to illustrate this type of measuring instrument. This questionnaire was designed to assess people's attitudes toward the control of drinking drivers and represents measurement on an ordinal scale. In this case the subjects themselves implement the measurement by checking a

For the following items, please put an "X" in the category that best describes your feelings about each particular item.

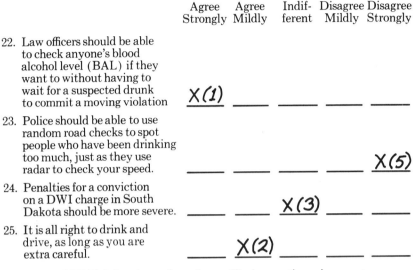

	Agree Strongly	Agree Mildly	Indif- ferent	Disagree Mildly	Disagree Strongly
22. Law officers should be able to check anyone's blood alcohol level (BAL) if they want to without having to wait for a suspected drunk to commit a moving violation	X(1)				
23. Police should be able to use random road checks to spot people who have been drinking too much, just as they use radar to check your speed.					X(5)
24. Penalties for a conviction on a DWI charge in South Dakota should be more severe.			X(3)		
25. It is all right to drink and drive, as long as you are extra careful.		X(2)			

FIGURE 2.4. A portion of an attitude questionnaire representing a measuring instrument providing ordinal scale data. Each subject check mark will be transformed to a numeric measure from 1 (agree strongly) through 5 (disagree strongly).

category representing their attitude about each item. With this type of measuring instrument, the researcher ordinarily transforms the subject's check mark for each question into a numeric value representing ordinal scale measurement. In this case to each item for which the "agree strongly" category is checked, the number 1 might be assigned, while a 5 would be assigned to a check under the "disagree strongly" column. It is also possible, of course, to obtain interval or ratio scale measurements from questionnaires or interview protocols. For example, a questionnaire item asking the subject to indicate his age would represent ratio scale measurement. Again, however, the implementation of the measurement is initiated by the subject himself.

Time-related aspects of behavior are frequently stipulated as the dependent variables in behavioral science investigations, particularly in psychology. A dependent variable such as running speed is measured, of course, by dividing the distance traveled by the time taken to travel it. Thus, the psychologist measuring the running speed of rats could measure the length of his maze and record elapsed time with something as simple as a stopwatch. One would be unlikely to find a psychologist content to measure the running speed of his rats in this manner, however. The reason is that measuring running speed in this fashion would tend to produce a highly unreliable measure of the dependent variable as well as being a tedious and time-consuming way of collecting data. The reaction time of the experimenter (the time between the experimenter's perception of the rat's starting to run and starting the stopwatch together with the time between his perceiving that the rat had reached the goal and stopping the watch) would tend to contaminate the ratio scale data produced by this measuring instrument. To avoid this problem, the psychologist would probably choose a more automatic timing method. He might, for example, set up his maze so that when the rat left the start box it would break the beam of a photocell and automatically start the timer. Similarly, when it reached the goal box it would break the beam of another photocell to stop the clock.

Additional complexities confront the behavioral scientist whose dependent variables are behavioral processes, or the effects of such processes, that cannot be directly observed and recorded. In some psychological and physiological studies, for example, the behavior of interest is the activity of various bodily organs or of the nervous system of the research subject. Obviously, the researcher cannot himself observe and record this activity, nor can the subject report the activity to the researcher by completing a questionnaire or an interview. The polygraph is widely used to measure and record these types of dependent variables. With this instrument it is possible to record a wide variety of psychophysiological measures, such as heart rate, respiration rate, and electrical resistance of the skin. These measures are associated with the responses of research subjects to stress as well as with such otherwise unobservable behavioral phenomena as attention and alertness.

The complexity of data-acquisition systems is probably as frequently a function of the researcher's desire to automate the data-recording process as it is a function of the actual process of quantifying observations. The principal justification for the use of sophisticated measurement systems to automate measuring and recording behavior is the large number of observations that must be made and the short time allowed for their recording. In many studies the number of separate measures of behavior that must be collected is too large to use simple paper-and-pencil recording techniques. In other instances these measurements must be made so rapidly that the researcher could not keep up with the recording process if he were forced to read measurements from timers or counters and record them manually.

The Highway Safety Research Vehicle is an instrumentation system designed to measure a number of factors in a driver's operation of a motor vehicle. Dependent variables measured with this system include number of fine steering adjustments per minute, number of gross steering adjustments per minute, number of speed changes per minute, number of brake applications, average speed of the vehicle (computed once each minute), the driver's heart rate, and the driver's galvanic skin response (GSR, a measure sensitive to stress and attentiveness). Each of these measures requires the use of a particular measuring instrument, or sensor, since none of these dependent variables is directly observable by the experimenter. These measures could, of course, be displayed to the researcher on counters, or meters, and he could manually record the data displayed to him each minute. Because there are so many separate measures, however, forcing the experimenter manually to record measures of each dependent variable at this rate could certainly produce unreliable data, since it would be virtually impossible for the experimenter to keep up with his recording task. As an alternative to this demand upon the researcher, the HSRV system provides that each of the measures of the various dependent variables be automatically recorded on a magnetic tape recorder located in the trunk of the car. These data are subsequently read directly into a computer, which then analyzes the data on each research subject. This automated measuring and recording system thereby frees the researcher to attend to other aspects of the subject's performance.

RELIABILITY AND VALIDITY

Up to this point we have been concerned with the mathematical meaning of various types of measures of behavior. We have seen that the scale of measurement on which our measures of the dependent variable or variables are based dictates the amount of information that can be obtained through the measurement process, and we have discussed several techniques used to summarize statistically our behavioral measures. Let us now consider two extremely important characteristics of good measurement, *reliability* and *validity*.

Reliability

The reliability of a behavioral measure is an index of the degree to which it consistently measures the same attribute and is related to the precision of the measuring instrument. A precise, or reliable, measure will give exactly the same reading on different occasions provided that the attribute being measured does not vary in value. For example, a reliable thermometer will always read 50° when the temperature to which it is exposed is 50°. If the thermometer one time shows a reading of 50°, another time 49°, and still another time 51° when the real temperature of the room has not changed, the device is unreliable, and the measurement of temperature obtained contains *error of measurement*. We can think of a given measure of the variable of interest, in this case temperature, as being of the following form:

$$X = T + e$$

where X is the obtained score, T is the true score, and e is an error component. Consider the case in which the true temperature of the room is 50° and the thermometer reading is 49°. Now X is 49°, the obtained reading; T is 50°, the real temperature; and e is $-1°$, the error component of the obtained score. Thus, $49° = 50° + (-1°)$.

We can also speak of variance in connection with both components of the obtained score. S_t^2, or the variance of the true score component, is an indication of the variability of the attribute being measured. If the actual temperature of the room changes from time to time, we would expect this change to be reflected in the obtained measure, X. The other variance component of our obtained measure involves changes in the size of the error component of X. Thus, if on one occasion the error component is $-1°$, on a second occasion $0°$, and on still another occasion $+1°$, the obtained X value will vary in size independently of the true score component. Therefore, we can also write $S_X^2 = S_t^2 + S_e^2$ to indicate that the variance observed in X from observation to observation is the sum of the *real variance* of the attribute measured and the *error variance* associated with each observation.

In the application of measurement, we of course want our measuring instrument to be sensitive to true score variance, so that if there is a 5° change in room temperature, our thermometer will show the change. On the other hand, we want to eliminate or reduce the error variance associated with the measure to increase its reliability. Two basic types of measurement errors may influence the obtained measurement of X. First, we may observe a *systematic error*, in which the obtained measure is always off by a constant amount. If, for example, our thermometer always read 1° low, so that when the actual temperature is 50° it shows 49°, we can say that the thermometer has a *constant error* of 1°. It should be noted that, in the case of this constant error of 1°, the error variance (S_e^2) would be zero, since the 1° error would be true of all measures taken with the thermometer. This type of error is not particularly damaging to the thermometer as a measuring instrument as long as the error is identified and we are aware of the bias introduced by the error.

On the other hand, our measuring instrument may be subject to the second type of error, or *random error*, in which the error variance is some amount greater than zero and the size of the error component of the obtained score varies from observation to observation. In this event we can never be sure just how large the error component of the obtained measurement is, and the reliability of the measure will be reduced in proportion to the size of the error variance. A more detailed discussion of variance can be found in the Appendix.

The reliability of a measuring instrument can be assessed in a variety of ways, most of which use the descriptive statistic of *correlation*. Correlation is a measure of the degree of relationship between two sets of measures. The correlation coefficient (r) may range from $+1.0$ to -1.0. A high positive correlation indicates that two measures are directly related to each other, while a large negative r indicates a strong inverse relation. Only when the correlation approaches zero do we speak of the two measures as being unrelated. Correlation is treated in more detail in the Appendix. We will briefly discuss a few of the procedures for obtaining estimates of reliability.

Test-Retest Reliability.   One common means of estimating the reliability of a measure is to employ the test-retest method. This technique is particularly suited to evaluating the reliability of tests. In this method a group of individuals is given the test on two separate occasions, and the scores obtained on the two occasions are subjected to a correlational analysis. The correlation coefficient (r) is then the index of the test's reliability. A high r (approaching $+1.0$ or -1.0) would indicate that the test is reliable or that the same attribute was measured on both occasions; a low correlation coefficient (approaching zero) would suggest that the test did not measure the same attribute on both occasions and that a significant amount of error variance is present.

Although the test-retest method is frequently employed and often serves as a useful method of assessing reliability, it does have some drawbacks. The most critical involves the time interval between the two administrations of the test. On the one hand, if this interval is too short, the subjects are likely to remember the test items and their responses on the first test when they take the second one. If this is the case, the correlation is likely to be spuriously high and the reliability of the test overestimated. On the other hand, if the test-retest interval is too long, the characteristics being measured may have changed between administrations, thus producing a change in the true score component of the obtained score from one testing to the other. In this case the reliability of the test is likely to be underestimated because part of the variance observed in the obtained scores from one administration to the other would be the result of true score variance rather than simply error variance.

Alternate Form and Alternate Observer Reliability. Another means of assessing the reliability of a test or measure of behavior involves the administration of two alternate forms of the same test or measure. If, for example, we intend to determine the reliability of an intelligence test, we could construct two forms of the same test and administer both forms to the same subjects. We would then correlate the data from the two tests and take the resulting correlation coefficient as an index of test reliability. This approach avoids the difficulty associated with the influence of the test-retest time interval on the correlation.

Closely parallel to the alternate form reliability technique is a method frequently used to determine the reliability of two observers. It is possible to determine a correlation between two observers who rate the same individuals. We can take the correlation coefficient obtained when two supervisors, for example, rate the performance of the same group of workers as an index of reliability; this correlation indicates the extent to which the supervisors' ratings agree, or measure the same attributes of the employees. Again, in either the alternate form or the alternate observer reliability method, the index of reliability is taken to be the correlation coefficient, with a high correlation indicating high agreement, or reliability, and a low correlation indicating unreliability.

Validity

Another important characteristic of a behavioral measure is its validity, or the extent to which it measures what it was designed to measure. There are a number of types of validity, some of which require statistical operations for their determination and some of which do not.

Face Validity. The simplest type of validity is a nonstatistical concept called face validity. Simply stated, face validity is the degree to which a measure appears to measure the attribute or behavior it is supposed to measure. If we are designing a test to measure the aptitude of horticulturists, for example, we could ensure high face validity by including in our test items on flowers, herbs, and vegetables. This form of test validity is not measured by statistical means and concerns only the superficial appearance of the measuring instrument. Face validity does assume some importance, however, in assuring the acceptance of the measuring instrument. Most people are probably more likely to use an instrument or test that at least appears to measure what they are interested in measuring.

Content Validity. Another nonstatistical type of validity is the extent to which a test covers the content area it is intended to cover. This type of validity is most often discussed with reference to achievement tests. The instructor of a course may, for example, be concerned that the tests he gives adequately sample the material he has covered in his lectures. To accomplish this purpose, he may systematically ask questions from each area covered to ensure some degree of content validity.

Predictive Validity. One of the most important types of validity for any type of behavioral measure is predictive validity. Predictive validity is the extent to which a given measure predicts performance on a criterion measure, and is statistically estimated by, once again, the correlation coefficient. Suppose, for example, that we wish to validate a test of scholastic aptitude. We might administer the test to a group of new freshmen at the beginning of an academic year and then collect grade point averages for the same individuals at the end of the academic year. We would then calculate the correlation between the test and the criterion measure (grade point average) and use the resulting correlation as an index of the test's validity. The more predictable the criterion is from the predictor measure, the higher the correlation coefficient, and thus the validity of the measure.

Concurrent Validity. In many situations it is either inconvenient or impossible to structure our determination of validity so that a definite time relationship exists between predictor and criterion, as is required with predictive validity. In these situations we can use a criterion measure collected at the same time as the measure we wish to validate. Suppose, for example, that we have a new IQ test that we have statistically compared with an established test. We can view the established IQ test as the criterion measure and the new test as the predictor measure. If the correlation coefficient indicates that the two tests are measuring the same attribute (a high correlation), we can take this finding as an index of the validity of the test.

Although some discussions of validity of measurement tend to use exclusively as examples various types of standardized tests, it should be kept in mind that validity is important in every behavioral measure. In many instances, however, the behavioral measure selected for observation is not subjected to the statistical evaluation required to determine predictive or concurrent validity. In some cases a simpler form of validity evaluation is perfectly suitable. If we are interested in the reaction time of subjects to the onset of a stimulus, for example, the appropriate dependent variable is obviously the elapsed time between stimulus and response. This measure has a high degree of face validity and of content validity, and most investigators would be satisfied with these nonstatistical types of validity measurement in this situation. Occasionally, however, researchers pay too little attention to the concept of validity of performance measures and consequently compromise the quality and meaningfulness of their research. It is not uncommon to find research reports on driver performance, for example, suggesting that a simple measure, such as reaction time or number of traffic cones knocked over, is an adequate and valid measure of driving skill. Much more uncommon are reports that systematically evaluate the validity of the performance measures used. The same is true of many other areas in the behavioral sciences. Though some measures, such as reaction time, do not require a detailed evaluation to determine their validity, many behavioral measures should be examined much more rigorously than they are. This is particularly true of performance measures that purport to assess complex behavioral processes.

SUMMARY

Dependent variables are aspects of research subjects' behavior that are measured in behavioral studies, whereas independent variables are characteristics of the experimental conditions or of the subjects themselves whose effects on the dependent variable or variables are assessed.

One of the most important aspects of research is the quantification or measurement of the dependent variable. Different scales of measurement depend on the rules that govern the ways in which numbers are assigned to observations of behavior.

Nominal scale measurement involves the determination of the equality of observations and is accomplished by simply categorizing the observations. Ordinal scale measurement adds to this process the concept of the amount of an attribute and thus conveys information about how observations can be ranked. Interval scale measures possess these qualities as well as equal intervals between the numeric categories on the measurement scale. Ratio scale measures possess all the attributes of interval measurement plus a zero point.

Descriptive statistics are means of summarizing observations of behavior. Behavioral observations can be summarized graphically through frequency distributions; single summary statistics, such as the mode, median, and mean, summarize pertinent characteristics of the frequency distributions. The measures of mode, median, and mean are kinds of averages that convey information about the central tendency of a distribution of scores.

Measuring instruments in behavioral research permit the organization and quantification of observations. These instruments range in complexity from a simple paper-and-pencil check list to a sophisticated computer-controlled measurement system.

To be useful, measurement of the dependent variable should be both reliable and valid. Reliability is the capacity of a measuring instrument to provide repeatable, or consistent, measurement of the behavior of interest and is related to the precision of the measuring instrument. Validity is the capacity of an instrument to measure what it was designed to measure.

3

SELECTION
AND ASSIGNMENT
OF RESEARCH SUBJECTS

In the previous chapter we discussed measurement, which is involved in any investigation in the behavioral sciences. We might say in a nutshell that the discussion centered on "what to observe" in a study. The topic of the present chapter is also common to all types of behavioral research and is concerned with "whom to observe." In this chapter we will consider the kinds of decisions behavioral scientists are faced with in determining what kinds of research subjects to observe, how to select individuals for observation, how to assign them to experimental groups, and how to generalize from studies based on the performance of small samples of individuals to the populations from which these samples were selected.

TYPES OF RESEARCH SUBJECTS

Behavioral scientists have conducted research on a tremendous variety of organisms. Research subjects in the behavioral sciences range from simple single cell organisms to extremely complicated human social organizations. At least a token appreciation of the variety of species whose behavior is systematically observed can be gained by considering a few examples:

44

Case 3.1. Thompson and McConnell (1955) used planaria, or flatworms, as research subjects in an investigation designed to determine whether simple conditioning can occur in an organism with such an elementary nervous system. These investigators attempted to condition, or establish an association between, electric shock and light by pairing the presentation of the two stimuli. The researchers found that under certain conditions the planaria could learn to associate the two stimuli and that they would, after the two stimuli had been paired, avoid the light as much as they would the shock.

Case 3.2. Harlow and Harlow (1965) conducted a number of studies designed to assess the development of affection in infant monkeys. In one study these investigators assessed the effects of age on the expression of affection as manifested by clinging behavior, in which the young monkey holds tightly to its mother. A definite pattern was found in the frequency with which this clinging occurred during the infant monkey's first 90 days of life. It might be noted that in this study a simple nominal scale measure of the dependent variable was used.

Case 3.3. In an interesting consolidation of several studies, Bitterman (1970) compared the performance of an unusual variety of animal species on a discrimination learning problem that assessed the effects of reinforcement (the independent variable) on responses to one of two "correct" stimuli. By adapting the testing situation to suit each species' response capabilities, Bitterman was able to compare the following different types of organisms: earthworm, cockroach, fish, turtle, pigeon, rat, and monkey. He found that two types of response patterns can be demonstrated, with the monkeys, rats, pigeons, and turtles showing one pattern of learning and the earthworms, cockroaches, and fish a distinctly different one.

Case 3.4. Olson and Davis (1964) compared the problem-solving capabilities of individuals and four-person groups. The dependent variable in this study was the proportion of correctly solved arithmetic problems. The investigators found that the performance of the groups was consistently superior to the performance of individuals and concluded that the superiority was due to the organizational characteristics of the group, which allowed the group members to pool their talents.

Although the few studies we have cited serve to illustrate the wide variety of organisms subjected to scientific examination, a comprehensive review of potential behavioral research subjects would fill several volumes much larger than this one. What should be kept in mind, however, is that whatever the species of the research subject or the scientific discipline of the researcher, a number of common characteristics can be observed. In virtually every type of behavioral study, a *sample* of research subjects is selected from a *population*, subjects are *assigned* to experimental conditions, and the experimenter attempts to *generalize* the results of his observations of the behavior of the sample of research subjects to the population they represent. These general characteristics of populations and samples and the procedures for selecting samples and assigning subjects will be discussed in the remainder of this chapter.

POPULATION VERSUS SAMPLE

Virtually every study attempts to provide information that can be generalized, or applied, to a particular population of individuals. In this context "population"[1] refers to the entire set of individuals of interest. If, for example, we were conducting a study to predict the outcome of a presidential election in the United States, the set of individuals in whom we would be interested is the population of eligible voters. We would not be interested in 12- to 17-year-olds, since they are not eligible to vote in a presidential election. Similarly, we would not be interested in prison inmates, who also are not eligible voters. The population in this case includes only those who are legally eligible to vote, but it includes every United States citizen in this category. The most accurate way to conduct our study of voter preference would, of course, be to interview every member of the population we have described and determine the preference of each. When we consider the immense amount of time and money that would be involved in this task, however, we might be willing to settle for a sample selected from the population. If the sample was chosen properly, it would be an unbiased representation of the population, and we could estimate the behavior of the population from the data obtained from the sample. This is, in fact, how the political pollsters conduct their business. Relatively small samples of individuals are carefully selected to represent the electorate accurately, and the data obtained from interviews of the sample group are used to predict or estimate the behavior of the population.

Although the population of interest in our voter preference study is very large, it is nonetheless finite and specifiable, so that we could obtain information on the exact size of the population. In other cases the researcher may attempt to generalize his results to a nonspecifiable and theoretical population. Assume, for example, that a study is conducted on the effects of noise on the automobile driver's performance. The researcher may wish to generalize his findings to a population consisting of

---

[1]In a more precise statistical sense the term "population" is used to refer to the set of numbers representing the behavioral characteristic of interest exhibited by the larger group. Similarly, "sample" refers to the subset of these numbers examined in a particular study.

all past, present, and future automobile drivers. In this case the population is infinite, so that its exact size cannot be specified. Many behavioral investigations are of this type; the population of interest consists of "people in general," and the intent of the investigator is to describe or evaluate "universal" principles or processes.

In either case, however, the manner in which the sample of objects, events, or individuals is selected from the population of interest will determine the legitimacy of the generalizations made on the basis of the research. A great many strategies have been developed to aid the behavioral scientist in sample selection. We will discuss a few of these strategies here.

SAMPLE SELECTION

There are two basic classes of sample selection in behavioral science research. These are *nonprobability* sampling techniques and *probability* sampling techniques. Each class contains a number of different sampling procedures.

Nonprobability Sampling Techniques

The various nonprobability sampling techniques are the most arbitrary of the sampling strategies we will discuss and are the most limited for the purpose of making generalizations from sample to population.

Incidental Samples. Perhaps the most common of the nonprobability sampling methods is the *incidental,* or *accidental,* sample. This method of sample selection is most frequently used in laboratory research. The principal rule used in selecting a sample of individuals for study with this strategy is to take whomever is available. Students in introductory behavioral science courses are frequently exposed to this sampling technique when they are asked to participate in research projects on a voluntary basis or told to participate as a part of their course requirements. Perhaps the most exhaustively tested population of individuals, with the possible exception of the white rat, is the college sophomore.

The primary advantage of this means of sample selection is that it is economical of the experimenter's time and resources. However, using incidental samples has a number of disadvantages. First, it is difficult, and in some cases impossible, to define adequately the population that this type of sample represents. We have no way of knowing, for instance, the frequency with which the type of individual volunteering for a particular study occurs in the population to which we wish to generalize our results. In other words, we cannot determine from an arbitrary sample of this type whether the kinds of individuals included in the sample really are representative of the kinds of individuals making up the population. Suppose, for example, that we selected a sample for our political preference poll from individuals attending a John Birch Society meeting simply because this sample was easy to obtain. With all due respect to this organization, it is doubtful that the members' political opinions accurately reflect the preference of the population of the country as a whole. As a consequence of a *biased* sample of this type, our generalizations about political preference would be incorrect and the study invalid. The best we could do in this situation would be to restrict our generalizations to the subset of the population that the sample represents. We might be able to generalize our results to the population of John Birch Society members, but even this might be a questionable tactic because we have contacted only a single group of these individuals.

Additional problems with this sampling strategy center on the volunteer subject. Research comparing volunteers with nonvolunteers has shown that the two groups differ in a substantial number of personal characteristics (Rosenthal & Rosnow, 1969). This research finding suggests that it is not safe to assume that those who volunteer to participate in behavioral research projects are particularly representative of people in general.

Although there are a great many valid objections to the use of incidental samples, in many cases the researcher has no other feasible choice of a sampling strategy. As we indicated earlier, this is particularly true of laboratory investigations, in which the population of potential research subjects is limited. Nonetheless, the researcher who must select his sample in this manner should be aware of the limitations imposed by his selection procedure and should take whatever precautions he can in both the sample selection and the interpretation of his results.

One of the precautions the experimenter can take is to screen his subjects carefully and reject those who deviate widely from known characteristics of the population of interest. This preliminary screening process might involve detailed biographical questionnaires, physical examinations, psychological tests, and other forms of assessment. An apparently effective way to avoid some of the biases introduced by the exceptional characteristics of volunteer subjects is the use of monetary incentives to participate. It has been the authors' experience that paid volunteer subjects tend to exhibit fewer of the eccentricities characteristic of nonpaid volunteers. If the experimenter can afford to do so, paying research participants a nominal fee may enhance the generalizability of his research results.

Quota Sampling. Another nonprobability sampling strategy is *quota sampling*. In using this procedure, the experimenter divides the population into various natural subdivisions and selects his sample in such a way that the number of individuals or cases selected from each subgroup is proportional to the size of the subgroup in the population as a whole. The sample therefore consists of the same number of subsamples as there are subgroups in the population, and the relative sizes of the subdivisions in both sample and population are proportional. The individuals selected for each subsample are ordinarily selected as incidental samples, however. For example, if a researcher conducting a study of psychomotor performance was concerned that the variable of handedness might influence the generalizability of his results, he might decide to quota sample right-handed and left-handed subjects. If he knew that 15 percent of the population is left-handed and the remaining 85 percent right-handed, he could select a sample containing the same proportion of right-handed to left-handed individuals. It is important to note, however, that he would still use subjects who were readily available to him.

Probability Sampling Techniques

Nonprobability sampling techniques are, as we have seen, subject to the influence of a number of potential biases that in some instances can render the results of a research endeavor meaningless insofar as generalizations to a population are concerned. A number of sampling strategies have been developed, however, to overcome or control such biases. These techniques are designed to ensure that each element or individual in the population of interest has an equal chance of being included in the sample. When this condition is met, obtaining a representative sample and accurately estimating the characteristics of the population are more likely.

Simple Random Sampling. The most elementary form of probability sampling is *simple random sampling*. With this technique each individual in the population has an equal chance of being selected for the sample, and the selection of each individual is determined solely by the laws of chance. There are two basic rules for the use of this sampling technique. First, all the elements or individuals in the population must be capable of being identified and listed. Second, the selection procedure used must guarantee that each element is equally likely to be included in the sample. Suppose, for instance, that we wished to draw a random sample of ten from the United States Senate to estimate the Senate's opinion of some political decision. The first thing we would do would be to make a list of all 100 Senators. We might then seal each Senator's name in identical capsules and place the 100 capsules in a large container. After shaking the container vigorously to ensure that the capsules were thoroughly mixed, we could then have an assistant draw a capsule from the container, record the name, replace the capsule in the container, draw another name, and repeat this process until a list of ten names had been obtained. This procedure, called random sampling with replacement (that is, the names are replaced in the population after they are sampled) would ensure that each of the 100 individuals in the population had an equal chance of being selected. It is possible, however, that a particular name would be selected more than once with this procedure. To avoid this possibility, we could use random sampling without replacement and simply draw ten names from the container. Although this strategy would be more practical, each name would no longer have one chance in 100 of being selected; the first would have one chance in 100, the second one chance in 99, and the tenth one chance in 90. Ordinarily, however, if the population is large, this procedure will yield a reasonable approximation to a simple random sample.

A simple mechanical selection procedure such as the above is not particularly difficult to implement provided the size of the population is relatively small. Assume, however, that we wished to select a simple random sample of all the adults residing in our community. Unless the community is very small, it would be time consuming to seal each person's name in a capsule and use the drawing technique. Instead, we might decide to select every fiftieth name in the local telephone directory on the assumption that last names are relatively random characteristics of the population. But this selection strategy could be questioned on a number of points. First, we might question the assumption that names are randomly distributed and that no systematic bias would enter our sample by taking every fiftieth name. On this point we could be relatively safe, since it is unlikely that the alphabetic ordering of names in the telephone book introduces any systematic bias concerning the important characteristics of the population; and it may in fact be true that the alphabetic order of names is itself random. In deciding to use the telephone directory, we have, however, made an additional tacit assumption that might have a significant influence on the representativeness of our sample. We have assumed that the telephone directory contains a complete listing of our population. By using the telephone directory as our population list, we have excluded all those members of the population who either do not have telephones or have unlisted numbers. Depending on the size of this subgroup in the population, this fact would tend to bias our sample because these individuals do not have an opportunity to be included. Another source of bias introduced by the use of the telephone directory as our list of adults in the community has to do with the adult member of the household whose name is listed with the telephone number. Before the advent of the women's liberation movement, at least, convention dictated that the name of the male head of the household be used for the directory listings of families having such an individual. To the extent that this is still the case, our telephone directory list would under-represent the adult females in the community, and this might constitute an even more important bias than that introduced by those individuals who do not have telephones. As a consequence of those shortcomings, our telephone directory selection procedure would not yield a simple random sample of the population.

The important points to remember in simple random sampling are, again, that each individual in the population must be capable of being listed and that each must have an equal chance of inclusion. Alternative probability sampling techniques are available for those cases in which a comprehensive listing of the population is not feasible. Although these alternative techniques allow the researcher to circumvent the difficulties associated with listing the population, all the methods are based on this form of sample selection.

Stratified Sampling. *Stratified sampling* is quite similar to the nonprobability strategy of quota sampling. Here again, the population is divided into subgroups on the basis of existing information. Suppose, for example, that we were to conduct a study of the vocational interests of the students at a particular college. The population in this investigation would be the entire student body at the college. One variable providing a natural set of subdivisions of a student body is class rank. Assume that 40 percent of the students are freshmen, 30 percent sophomores, 20 percent juniors, and 10 percent seniors. Rather than listing the entire student body and randomly selecting a sample of the required size, we might wish to guarantee that similar proportions of each class rank appeared in the sample. To accomplish this purpose and still provide that each individual in the population had an equal chance to be represented, we would compile four separate lists of the individuals in each *stratum*, or class, and draw a random sample from each of the four *strata*. If our overall sample size was to be 100 students, we would select 40 freshmen from the list of all the freshman students attending the college. Similarly, we would select

30 students from the sophomore list, 20 from the junior list, and ten from the senior list. As the reader can see, the stratified sampling technique is just an extension of simple random sampling. Instead of one sample, we have selected four simple random samples from the student population. We are still required to compile a complete list of the population, but in this case the list is broken down into four distinct sections corresponding to the strata, or classes. With this method the number of individuals selected from each of the strata will be proportional to the distribution of individuals by class in the population, and each individual will have the same chance of being included in the sample as every other member of his class. Thus, the stratified sampling technique is merely a combination of quota and simple random sampling.

Area Sampling. In many research situations, particularly survey research, it is extremely difficult to obtain a list of all the members of a population. Yet it is still possible to select a random or probability sample of the individuals in a community, for instance, by using somewhat different techniques. One such technique is *area sampling*. In area sampling relatively fixed geographical characteristics of a community are used to allow the investigator to select a sample of individuals that is not subject to the biases associated with the use of incomplete lists of the target population. One geographic characteristic of most communities that can be used in area sampling is physically defined city blocks. If we were conducting a survey of a given community and wanted a random sample of the entire population of the community, we might use the geographic division of the city by blocks instead of compiling a detailed listing of the population. We might, for instance, compile a list of the city blocks and randomly choose a number of them as *sampling units* from which to select individuals for inclusion in the survey sample. Within each selected block we could then use a technique such as cluster sampling or even simple random selection to obtain our sample. With area sampling we are not selecting the individuals who will be included in the final sample but sampling units that contain these individuals. By randomly selecting these units and then providing for a probability sample of individuals within the units, we meet the requirement of providing each element or individual in the unit with an equal chance of being included in the final sample. Through random selection of a number of city blocks, each city block also has an equal chance of being a sampling unit.

Cluster Sampling. *Cluster sampling* is used by survey researchers to avoid the difficulties previously indicated in connection with compiling a complete list of the entire population. This sampling technique incorporates the features of simple random sampling and frequently includes area sampling. To illustrate this technique, let us again suppose that we wished to conduct some sort of survey in a particular community and required a random but economical sample of all the adults residing in that community. To accomplish this purpose in the most efficient manner, we would probably use a multistage cluster sampling technique. The first stages of this procedure would involve area sampling to select sampling units of a manageable size or *clusters*. As a first step we might divide the city into wards or precincts, geographical units that contain a number of city blocks and that ordinarily are roughly equivalent in population. From our list of precinct clusters, we would randomly select a few, again giving each precinct an equal chance of being selected. In the second step we would divide each of the precinct clusters into city blocks, or subclusters, list these sampling units, and again randomly select a number of city block subclusters from each precinct. We would then list the dwelling units in each city block and again perform a random selection to establish subclusters, or sampling units. Finally, we would randomly select the particular adult resident who is to receive the questionnaire or other survey measure. It is only at this final stage that the basic survey element, the individual adult resident, is involved; but each stage of the cluster sampling process has involved random selection procedures, which tend to eliminate biases toward the inclusion of any particular individual in the sample.

ASSIGNMENT TECHNIQUES

The probability sampling techniques we have discussed are most useful in survey research and are frequently not applicable to experimental research situations, in which, as we have indicated, the incidental sample is often the only procedure available to the researcher. The behavioral scientist using the experimental method of observation faces another set of problems that have a great deal in common with the problems of sample selection. As we shall see in subsequent chapters, the experimental method involves the assessment of the *effects of independent variables on dependent variables* in an experimentally controlled environment. In some cases the independent variables consist of different experimental treatments applied to different groups of subjects or to the same subjects on different occasions. Thus, the researcher must decide on a particular strategy for assigning the subjects to treatment groups or on methods of assigning treatments to subjects.

We saw, in our discussion of sample selection techniques, that systematic sampling biases can seriously affect the representativeness of our sample; similarly, systematic biases in the way that subjects are assigned to experimental conditions or groups can seriously affect the validity of experiments. The same general solution, randomization, is the key to the elimination of both types of bias. Assume, for example, that we were to conduct an experimental study to assess the effects of noise on the ability of subjects to perform an inspection task. We might decide to use two groups of subjects in this study, one to do the inspection task while noise was present (the treatment group) and the other in quiet (the control group). The validity of this study would depend on our ability to make sure that the only thing responsible for differences in performance between the two groups was the experimental treatment. If we selected a group of industrial quality-control inspectors for the noise group and a group of college freshmen for the control group, for instance, we would be quite likely to find differences in inspection performance in favor of the noise group. Here, however, it is probable that the variable contributing to the differences would be the inspection task experience of the subjects rather than the noise condition. To overcome this source of bias, the experimental researcher would use *random assignment* to experimental groups. This procedure is an exact corollary of simple random sampling. The experimenter would list all the subjects to be tested under all the conditions and randomly select individuals for each group from the list. A common means of effecting this random assignment is to use a *table of random numbers*. These tables, found in appendixes to most statistics texts, are simply lists of numbers generated in random fashion. Table 3.1 presents such a list.

Table 3.1 contains a total of 160 random digits arranged in ten rows and four columns, with each column containing a four-digit set. Each digit has been randomly determined independently of every other digit. Suppose that in our noise study we wished to test ten subjects in each of the two groups. After selecting our 20 subjects for the study, probably by means of an incidental sample, we would now use the table of random numbers to assign each of the 20 subjects to one or the other of the experimental groups. Our first task would be to make a complete list of the 20 subjects and assign a number from 1 to 20 to each individual. We would then use the table to select those individuals to be assigned to the noise group. To do so, we might start at the beginning of the table and split the first column into two columns of two-digit numbers. We would then work down the column and the subsequent columns of two-digit numbers until we have selected ten numbers from 01 through 20. The first five numbers in the first column (79, 55, 55, 45, and 47) are not used

TABLE 3.1.   An abbreviated table of random numbers.

	Column			
Row	*1*	*2*	*3*	*4*
1	79 83	95 50	87 75	36 08
2	55 24	78 44	15 72	(03) 12
3	55 50	(04)(07)	15 71	10 27
4	45 36	02 57	44 63	44 73
5	47 91	40 68	04 75	22 03
6	(15)(19)	49 (17)	92 80	57 89
7	(08) 31	92 53	44 31	24 60
8	(20) 98	(11) 97	63 24	72 92
9	70 86	65 80	96 71	74 01
10	53 (02)	84 81	63 73	23 72

because they are larger than 20. The first number selected for the noise group is 15, the second 08, the third 20, and so on. These ten subjects (02, 03, 04, 07, 08, 11, 15, 17, 19, and 20) would constitute the noise group, while the remaining subjects (01, 05, 06, 09, 10, 12, 13, 14, 16, and 18) would make up the control group. The assignment of subjects would be completely determined by chance in this situation, since the use of the random number table would ensure that each subject would have an equal chance of being assigned to either group.

While random assignment is an effective technique in eliminating systematic biases in experiments using different groups of subjects, other problems confront the researcher when he applies different experimental treatments to the same group of subjects on different occasions. In our noise study, for example, we might have chosen to test a single group of subjects once during quiet and another time in a noise condition rather than using two different groups. Although a repeated measures design (using the same subjects for all experimental conditions) has an advantage in that it avoids the problems of systematic differences between groups, it is subject to another difficulty in that one test session may influence subsequent tests of the same subjects. In our inspection task study, for example, the subjects might acquire a significant amount of learning during the first test session, and this learning would improve their performance in the second session regardless of the influence of the independent variable (noise). Thus, if we tested all the subjects first under the quiet condition and second under noise, the effects of practice might tend to hide the effects of the noise on their performance. To overcome this difficulty, we could once again resort to randomization. This time, however, we could randomize the order of occurrence of the two testing conditions, so that the order in which they occurred would not systematically bias the results. To do this with just two test conditions is a very simple process. We might, for example, flip a coin for each subject to determine the condition he will be tested under in the first session and use the noise condition if the coin comes up heads, the quiet condition if the coin comes up tails. Again, the random selection of treatment order accomplishes exactly the same purpose as does simple random sampling and simple random assignment to groups; it guarantees that each treatment order has an equal chance of occurring for a given subject and thus eliminates the introduction of systematic bias in the results.

SAMPLING AND ASSIGNMENT PROBLEMS WITH ANIMAL SUBJECTS

As we have pointed out, animals are often used as subjects in behavioral studies. In fact, the albino rat has become well established as the standard laboratory animal in behavioral research, and a significant percentage of all studies published uses this species. Although our discussion of sampling and assignment of subjects until now has been concerned with human subjects, much of what we have said is also applicable to other species. However, the investigator using subhuman subjects encounters some unique problems. Some of the problems, of course, are species specific; and if we were to attempt to discuss all the different species that behavioral scientists use, we would require a number of volumes for adequate coverage. Consequently, in this section we will be primarily concerned with some of the problems encountered by investigators who study the albino variant of the brown rat *(Rattus norvegicus)*.

In most cases a researcher interested in studying some aspect of the albino rat's behavior orders his subjects from one of a number of suppliers. Generally, when ordering, the investigator specifies the strain, sex, and age of the animals. Sometimes he even orders animals that have had certain types of surgery. However, as Sidowski and Lockard (1966) point out:

> Freshly received animals are not uniform products from an automatic production line, nor are they a random sample from the world's

population of rats. Animal suppliers differ greatly in such environmental practices as the ambient temperature, light-dark cycle, type of food, cage size and animal density, and the physical arrangement of food and water devices.... Since different animal suppliers employ different combinations of conditions, the same designated strain purchased from different suppliers is not a homogeneous population because of the different effects of the two environments [pp. 8–9].

There are, then, a number of factors associated with what rats encounter while maturing that may affect their later behavior. Thus, one measure that a researcher may employ in obtaining research subjects is to make sure that all the animals come from the same supplier. As pointed out, using the same strain of rat from several suppliers will not ensure that they have had the same experiences prior to being shipped. Even rats of the same strain received from the same supplier at different times have not always encountered the same environmental conditions. For example, a particular shipment of rats is typically taken from the same large cage at the supplier's or at least from the same tier of cages. The tier of cages may be near the floor, where illumination is different from that of higher cages. Differences in temperature, noise, and so on may also exist.

In many studies the researcher is able to order all the subjects he will need in one shipment, thus solving to some extent the problem of differences in the animals' past experience. Sometimes, however, the facilities available to a researcher are not large enough to maintain all the animals needed for an experiment, so he must then have to depend on several shipments. In this case he would certainly want to use the same strain of rats each time and order them from the same supplier.

The same comments about random assignment of subjects to experimental groups hold true whether we are discussing rats or humans. Thus, the investigator would typically assign the rats he plans to use in his study to the various experimental conditions on a random basis, at least when the rats have been purchased from a supplier.

There are several alternatives to purchasing adult rats from a supplier for use in research. Sometimes an investigator will order very young rats and will raise them in his own laboratory until they are old enough for his research. This procedure assures that his subjects have been maintained in a standard and describable environment prior to testing. Some scientists breed their own research animals—although this is an expensive procedure in terms of space requirements. Since age is an important variable in rat research and since in most studies rats of nearly identical ages are used, it takes a large breeding facility to assure an investigator that on a given day he will have available 50 or 100 male rats of the same age. Consequently, most researchers rely on suppliers for their subjects.

There are some definite advantages, however, in breeding and raising one's own rats. Obviously, environmental conditions can be controlled, and, in terms of past experience, the rats used in a study would be nearly identical. Often investigators who raise their own animals do not rely on random assignment but instead use what is called a *split litter* technique. Assume that we have four litters of rats, each consisting of six males. Suppose that the experiment calls for a control group and two experimental groups. We would place two animals from each of the four litters in each of the three groups. Thus, each group would consist of a total of eight rats but would be equally represented by rats from each litter. This technique has several advantages, the primary one being that it assures the investigator that he has groups of comparable genetic constitution.

Much more could be said about the problems of subject selection and assignment with animals. The above, however, should serve to make an important point. Many investigators who work exclusively with human subjects often envy their colleagues who are "rat psychologists" because they assume that they have no problems of this sort. It should be apparent that this is not the case—the investigator working with rats must be just as concerned about selection and assignment if he hopes to have generalizable results as the investigator working with humans.

SUMMARY

Behavioral scientists have used a variety of subjects, ranging from flatworms to complex groups of humans, in behavioral investigations.

Most behavioral research attempts to generalize to a population of individuals on the basis of an intensive study of a sample of subjects drawn from that population.

Samples of individuals are selected from particular populations according to either probability or nonprobability sampling strategies. Both types of sampling techniques are intended to ensure that the selected sample will faithfully represent the characteristics of the population to which the results of the study are to be generalized.

Two common nonprobability sampling techniques are incidental sampling (in which subjects are readily available) and quota sampling (in which the researcher selects his sample to represent proportionately such natural subdivisions of the population as sex). These techniques do not assure representativeness in the sample and may fail to control sampling biases.

method because with it they can maintain the most control over the research situation. Other researchers feel that the experimental method has little value, since it introduces artificiality and is certain to lead to overlooking variables that may be very important. However, most behavioral scientists recognize that the experimental method has certain advantages over the other approaches and use it whenever an independent variable can be manipulated. But they also recognize that many important variables do not lend themselves to manipulation and, consequently, cannot readily be studied by the experimental method. The advantages and disadvantages of the various methods of studying behavior will be considered in this and the next chapter.

THE EXPERIMENTAL METHOD

As we have stated, the experimental method allows the experimenter the most control over the research situation. In this strategy the investigator manipulates or controls certain aspects of the situation (independent variables) and observes the behavior (dependent variables) for resultant changes.

In designing an experiment, the investigator must take so many factors into account that a complete discussion of all of them is far beyond the scope of this text. Indeed, graduate students in the behavioral sciences are required to take at least one course—often several—dealing exclusively with the topic of experimental design. We will discuss here only the basic considerations involved in the design of experiments and indicate some of the differences between a good and a poor research design.

Designing the Experiment

Kerlinger (1964) states, "Research design has two basic purposes: (1) *to provide answers to research questions* and (2) *to control variance*" (p. 265). Thus, the criterion for a good research design is whether the study answers the research question. To answer the question, the investigator must consider the manner in which he will control variance in his study. The kinds of variance with which he must be concerned and the techniques of control have been previously discussed and will be only touched upon in this chapter.

Among the many features of an experiment that must be considered to meet the criterion of a good research design, the investigator must pay particular attention to these: (1) the selection and measurement of the dependent variable, (2) selection and assignment of subjects, (3) manipulation of the independent variable, and (4) control of nuisance, or extraneous, variables.

Selection and Measurement of the Dependent Variable. This topic has been dealt with in detail earlier and will not be considered to any extent here. Although the dependent variable to be used is determined, at least in part, by the goals of the investigation, we shall see later in this chapter that the dependent variable is often a variable of convenience. In other words, it is selected not because it is relevant to the research question but because it is convenient to work with and measure. In the section on the relevance of laboratory studies to the real world, we shall see that selection of convenient dependent variables is one reason that often the results of laboratory studies are not generalizable to real world situations.

Selection and Assignment of Subjects. The procedures that the investigator follows in selecting his subjects and assigning them to his experimental conditions assure him that the groups of subjects exposed to the conditions are essentially equivalent. Thus, if he finds that the groups behave differently under the experimental conditions, he can be reasonably certain that these differences are due to the conditions and not to intersubject differences existing before the experiment. The importance of controlling intersubject differences through random selection and assignment was discussed in some detail in Chapter 3. As we noted, it is extremely difficult to select subjects in a truly random manner. However, it is less difficult to assign the subjects randomly to an experimental condition or group, and this procedure is usually followed in designing an experiment. A fundamental rule of good experimental design is to: *"Randomize whenever possible; select subjects at random; assign subjects to groups at random; assign experimental treatments to groups at random"* (Kerlinger, 1964, p. 299). Kerlinger goes on to state that "to the extent that randomization is ignored or is not possible, . . . research designs are weak" (p. 299).

In some experiments subjects are not assigned to experimental conditions on a purely random basis. Although an effort at random selection of the subjects for the experiment may have been made, the researcher may wish to *match* the subjects on the basis of certain characteristics before the experiment actually begins. The individual subjects can be matched on a number of such variables as age, sex, or intelligence that the investigator thinks may affect the dependent variable. The experimenter then has two groups of subjects with each subject in one group matched with a subject in the other group in age, sex, intelligence, or whatever other variable was used in the matching procedure.

Although the matching technique is frequently used and the researcher assumes that he has controlled for intersubject differences, it is important that the matching variable be relevant to the research purpose. For example, if there is no relation between age and the dependent variable involved, matching on the basis of age is of little value. The investigator may not know all the variables that are relevant for matching, but his knowledge of the field should allow him to reject a number of variables that he knows would not affect the dependent variable.

Another procedure for controlling intersubject differences is to use subjects as their own controls. With this technique a subject is assigned to each of the conditions of the experiment. For example, we may be investigating the effects of four levels of noise on reaction time. In one type of design (sometimes called a *between subjects design*), we would assign a separate group of subjects to each of the four noise conditions. However, by having all the subjects participate in each of the four conditions (called a *within subjects,* a *repeated measures,* or a *treatment by subjects design*), we can be more certain that the four treatment groups are equal in terms of subject variables. This technique may, however, introduce another problem if the *order* of the presentation of the noise conditions is not randomized. If all the subjects received the same order of treatments, the results might be influenced by practice or fatigue. For example, if noise level 1 was always presented first, noise level 2 second, and so forth, we could not be sure that by the time the subject was tested under noise condition 4, his performance might not be at least partially determined by his previous experience with the other noise conditions. Randomizing the order of presentation for each subject prevents this problem.

Subject selection and assignment is one of the most important aspects of experimental design. The difference between a good and a poor design is often the manner in which the subjects are selected and assigned to the experimental conditions.

Manipulation of the Independent Variable. In the experimental method the independent variable is manipulated in such a way that the subjects are exposed to experimental conditions representing two or more values of the independent variable. For example, if the independent variable in a study is noise, we might design the study so that the subjects are exposed to one of four different intensity levels. Earlier in the text some of the problems associated with proper measurement of the independent variable were discussed. It should be kept in mind that the selection of levels of independent variables is not just a haphazard procedure and may even require the investigator to conduct exploratory research.

The key feature of the experimental method, then, is that there are two or more values of the independent variable or variables and that the investigator determines whether the dependent variable varies systematically with the values of the independent variable. The investigator can manipulate the independent variable in a number of ways. Let us consider several examples.

Case 4.1. An investigator is interested in determining the effects of alcohol on reaction time. He randomly assigns his subjects to two groups. The subjects in one of the groups are given enough alcohol in a fruit juice mix so that at the end of one-half hour their blood-alcohol concentration (BAC) is at the .05 level. At this point they are tested on a reaction-time apparatus. The subjects in the second group receive the fruit juice mix without alcohol and are also tested at the end of one-half hour. The subjects do not know whether they received the alcohol drink or only fruit juice. The experimenter statistically compares the reaction times of both groups and finds that the reaction times of the subjects who received the alcohol are significantly slower than those of the subjects who did not.

The above is an example of the simplest type of experiment (sometimes referred to as a *preliminary design*). Only two values of the independent variable are represented—one above zero (the .05 blood-alcohol concentration) and one at zero (no alcohol in the blood). In this type of design, the group receiving the alcohol is referred to as the *experimental group*, while the subjects who did not receive alcohol make up the *control group*. The performance (dependent variable) of the subjects in the experimental group is compared with that of the subjects in the control group to determine whether the independent variable (blood-alcohol concentration) had any effect.

Although this type of design showed the investigator that alcohol has an effect on reaction time, it did not tell him a great deal about the relationship. To understand the nature of this relationship better, he might design a somewhat different study.

Case 4.2. Instead of assigning his subjects to only two groups, the experimenter assigns them to six groups. One is still a control group that receives only the fruit juice with no alcohol. However, the subjects in the other five groups receive enough alcohol to establish a .02, a .04, a .06, a .08, or a .10 BAC at the end of one-half hour. All the subjects are again tested on the reaction time apparatus one-half hour after receiving the drink.

With this design (called a *systematic* or *functional design*), a number of values of the independent variable are studied rather than only two, as was the case in the first example. A design of this type tells the investigator not only whether there is a relationship between the independent variable and the dependent variable but also something about the characteristics of the relationship. For example, many investigators in the area of alcohol research believe in the so-called linear deterioration hypothesis. This concept suggests that if a BAC of .06 produces a performance decrement, then a higher BAC will produce more impairment and a lower BAC less impairment. In the above study, because a number of different points along the BAC continuum were studied, the investigator would be able to draw some conclusions about the concept of linear deterioration that he would not be able to draw from the first study, in which only two points were used.

In both of these studies, the investigator was able to assess the effects of a single independent variable on a dependent variable. However, in many studies the investigator is interested in assessing the effects of several independent variables. This sort of study demands a design somewhat more complex (called a *factorial design*) than those of the previously discussed studies. Consider, for example, the following study.

Case 4.3. A researcher is interested in studying the performance of radar operators under a number of different conditions. The task required of the subjects in his experiment is to detect and report a signal consisting of a spot of light appearing for a very brief time on a cathode-ray tube. The performance measure (the dependent variable) is the percentage of signals detected in one hour. The investigator assesses the effects of signal intensity and signal frequency (the independent variables) on the dependent variable (percentage of correct detections) by using two levels of signal brightness (dim and bright) and two rates of signal presentation (fast and slow). With two levels of each independent variable, signal detection can be studied under four conditions. These are shown in Table 4.1. Note that the percentage of correct detections (dependent variable) can be determined with dim signals presented slowly, with bright signals presented slowly, and with dim and bright signals presented rapidly.

In this investigation the researcher was concerned with the *main effects* of two independent variables (signal intensity and signal frequency) on the dependent variable (percentage of signals detected). However, another important type of experimental effect occurs when several independent variables are involved in a study. This is called the *interaction* effect. If the statistical analysis of the data obtained from the study cited in case 4.3 revealed a significant interaction effect, the study would reveal an important fact to the investigator. It would tell him that

TABLE 4.1. The effect of signal intensity and signal frequency (independent variables) on signal detection (dependent variable). With two levels of signal intensity (dim and bright) and two levels of signal frequency (fast and slow), signal detection can be studied under four conditions. The percentage of correct detections can be determined with dim signals presented slowly, with bright signals presented slowly, and with dim or bright signals presented rapidly.

Independent Variable 2 (Signal Frequency)		*Independent Variable 1 (Signal Intensity)*	
		Dim	*Bright*
	Slow	Condition 1 Dim-Slow	Condition 2 Bright-Slow
	Fast	Condition 3 Dim-Fast	Condition 4 Bright-Fast

the effect of one independent variable (intensity, for example) on the dependent variable is different at different levels of the other independent variable. In other words, the effect of signal intensity at the dim level on signal detection may be different at the fast level of signal presentation from that at the slow level. Basically, an interaction can be thought of as "A relationship between independent variables such that their joint effect could not have been predicted from a knowledge of how each separately affected the dependent variable" (Arnoult, 1972, pp. 200–201).

In a study such as this, the investigator must make a number of decisions in addition to deciding how he will manipulate the independent variables. For example, he might randomly assign his subjects to four groups and then test one group under condition 1, a second group under condition 2, and so forth (a between subjects design). Analysis of his data would then reveal whether any significant differences existed among the four groups in the number of correct detections. However, he might also decide to test each of his subjects under each of the four conditions in a within subjects or treatment by subjects design. As pointed out previously, in this case he would randomize the order of presentation of the four conditions for each subject. In other words, all the subjects would not be tested under conditions 1, 2, 3, and 4 in that order. One subject might follow a 4, 3, 2, 1 sequence, another a 3, 1, 4, 2 sequence, and so forth. If the conditions are not randomly assigned, a systematic bias might be introduced in which testing under condition 1 affects performance on condition 2, which in turn affects performance on condition 3, and so forth.

Both approaches—assigning a group of subjects to each condition or each subject to all conditions—have their advantages and disadvantages. In general, the latter method provides the best matching of experimental groups, although in many experimental situations this design is not feasible. The number of potential independent variables is, of course, virtually limitless, and the manner in which they are manipulated depends on the objectives of the study. The next chapter discusses other kinds of independent variables that are frequently employed with nonexperimental research methods. The important thing to remember, however, is that when the experimental method is employed, the independent variables must be manipulated in some fashion to determine whether these manipulations result in changes in the dependent variable.

Control of Nuisance Variables.   If the research design is a good one, the investigator will be able to conclude that the independent variables are responsible for any experimental effects demonstrated. To draw this conclusion safely, however, he must be certain that no other aspects of the experimental situation affect the dependent variable.

Any experimental situation typically contains a number of variables in whose effects the investigator is not interested but that may have an effect on the dependent variable. These are called *extraneous* or *nuisance* variables, and it is essential that the researcher design his study in such a fashion that these variables do not affect his results.

One method that the investigator might employ is the *hold constant* approach, in which the extraneous variable or variables are held constant over all experimental conditions. For example, in our signal detection study, it might be expected that such variables as room temperature, light, and noise level could have an effect on the dependent variable. The experimenter would make certain that all these variables were held constant during the experiment, so that all subjects in all groups would be tested under the same temperature, light, noise, and so forth. Similarly, the investigator would make certain that all the subjects received identical instructions, were tested at approximately the same time of day, and, if possible, were tested by the same experimenter. In other words, all the subjects would be treated in an identical fashion except for the difference associated with the manipulation of the independent variable.

Another method of controlling extraneous variables has already been mentioned. In discussing the signal detection study, we pointed out that if a treatment by subject design (each subject tested under each experimental condition) is used, the order of presentation of the experimental conditions to each subject must be randomized. Thus, one subject might be tested under condition 4 first, then 2, then 3, and then 1, another subject might be tested in a 3, 1, 4, 2 sequence, and so forth. Doing so eliminates the possible effect of the order of presentation (an extraneous variable) on the results. By assigning all subjects to all conditions (a control method called systematic variation), intersubject differences are systematically varied. This controls another extraneous variable.

There are other methods, some quite technical, of eliminating or controlling nuisance variables. Regardless, however, of the manner in which the investigator deals with them, the confidence that he can place in the results of his investigation depends to a great extent on adequate control of these variables.

We have briefly considered four essential features of good experimental design. To the degree that the experimenter has carefully selected and measured his dependent variable, controlled intersubject differences, manipulated his independent variable or variables, and controlled extraneous variables, he will have answered the research question that he set out to answer.

The Control of Variance

Earlier in the chapter we pointed out that an important purpose of research design is to control variance. Essentially, the term "variance" as used here refers to the variability of the measures obtained of the dependent variable during an experiment.

The experimenter is concerned with three kinds of variance when designing an experiment. These can be called *experimental* variance, *extraneous systematic* variance, and *error* variance. Experimental variance, in general, is the variance introduced into the dependent variable by the independent variables being manipulated. The experimenter attempts to maximize this type of variance. To do so, he makes his experimental conditions as different as possible, thus using values of the independent variable that are reasonably different. An important function, then, of the manipulation of the independent variables is maximizing experimental variance.

On the other hand, the experimenter wants to be sure that he is measuring experimental variance, not variance due to extraneous variables. Thus, in his design he attempts to control extraneous systematic variance that might affect the dependent variable by following the procedure already discussed. He randomizes subject selection and assignment and experimental treatments whenever possible, and he either eliminates or controls other extraneous variables.

If a subject is tested in a number of trials during an experiment, his responses will vary from one trial to another. The subject may guess, may not be paying attention during one or more trials, may get tired momentarily, and so forth. Variation of responses during an experimental session results in errors of measurement and is the most common source of error variance, which is essentially an unpredictable or random type of variance. The investigator attempts to minimize error variance by carefully controlling the various conditions of the experiment. He may also try to minimize error variance by increasing the reliability of his measures. With an increase in reliability, the measures are less likely to fluctuate randomly, so that error variance is reduced.

An Example of a Faulty Design

To illustrate an experimental design that would not answer the research question and would not control variance, we will consider an example having a number of design flaws. Though a study this poorly designed is not apt to be found in the scientific literature, reported studies with some of the flaws discussed here are not uncommon.

Case 4.4. The question that the investigator wished to answer was "Do amphetamines (bennies) have an effect on driver performance?" Since the research was to take place in a laboratory on a college campus, the investigator decided to use college students for his subjects. He was teaching an introductory psychology course and informed his students that as part of the course requirement, they would have to take part in his or someone else's experiment. However, since he needed only 30 subjects, he explained the purpose of his study to the class and asked for volunteers. The first 30 students (males and females) who volunteered were accepted. They were told to report to the laboratory at any time during a one-week period.

As his measure of driver performance, the researcher decided to use a reaction time test. In this test the subject viewed a panel that contained a red light. When the red light went on, the subject depressed a telegraph key located directly in front of him. The reaction time (dependent variable) was the amount of time between the onset of the light and the depression of the telegraph key.

The researcher decided to use three experimental conditions in his study. In one of the conditions, the subjects would receive one benny, in another two bennies, and in the third condition three bennies. The first ten subjects to report to the laboratory were tested under the first condition, the second ten under the second condition, and the last ten under the third condition.

When a subject reported to the laboratory, either the researcher or one of his graduate assistants gave the subject the drug. If there were several subjects available at the same time, they were all given the drug, and then one was taken immediately to the test room and the reaction time testing conducted. The test took 30 minutes. Then the next subject was tested. All ten of the subjects in the one-benny condition were tested on the first day. However, it took the rest of the week to test the subjects in the other two conditions because it was necessary to remind them in class that they had "volunteered" and that if they did not show up for the study they would not complete the course.

The week selected for the study was in early August, and the laboratory was not air conditioned. During the first day, when the one-benny subjects were tested, the laboratory temperature was 90°. However, an unusual cold spell appeared during the remainder of the week, and the laboratory temperature was 70° during the remaining test sessions.

After testing all the subjects, the researcher subjected his data to a statistical analysis to determine whether the differences in reaction time shown among the subjects under the three experimental conditions were significant. He found that the differences were not significant and concluded that amphetamines do not have an effect on driver performance.

Obviously, the design that the investigator used in the above study does not answer the question "Do amphetamines (bennies) have an effect on driver performance?" Let us consider the reasons that it does not and some of the steps the investigator might have taken to improve the design.

First, the manner in which the researcher obtained subjects for his study is unsatisfactory. Because he restricted his sample of subjects to those from an introductory psychology class, his findings would be generalizable only to similar individuals in other introductory psychology classes even if they were randomly selected, which they were not. However, random selection from the class would have eliminated another possible source of bias that is often involved when volunteers are used in research. The students that volunteered may have been atypical in many respects. Several studies have shown that the person who volunteers for a psychological study for no other reason than to take part in the study may differ from nonvolunteers in a number of ways.

This, of course, presents the investigator with a dilemma. If he randomly selected subjects and required them to take part in the experiment, the ethical question of subject coercion, which was discussed in Chapter 1, would be raised. In fact, by informing the class that they would be required to take part in an experiment as part of the course requirements, he already used a form of coercion. If he relied strictly on volunteers, he would encounter the problem mentioned above. A partial solution would have been to obtain a random list of names from among the students in the class and then ask each student on the list if he or she would be a subject in the study.

The first major flaw, then, is the manner in which subjects were selected. Note that the investigator also made no attempt at randomly assigning the subjects to one of the three experimental conditions. Rather, the ten subjects who arrived first were tested under the first condition; when the tests under this condition were completed, arriving subjects were assigned to the second condition; and so forth. Moreover, no effort was made to match for sex. All the subjects in the first condition could have been women, while the subjects in the remaining groups might have been mixed or all men. Even without random selection of subjects, an effort to assign the subjects to the experimental conditions randomly would have helped. The manner in which the subjects were selected and assigned in no way assured the investigator that his groups were equivalent. Thus, he did not control intersubject differences.

The manipulation of the independent variable is another major flaw in the design. In each of the experimental conditions, the subjects received some drug, so that there was no control group (a group receiving no drugs). In addition to a control group, it would have been desirable to have a *placebo group*, one that was given pills that looked like bennies but were known to have no behavioral effects. Just the fact that the subjects took pills may have modified their behavior to some extent, even if the drug had no real effects, and a placebo group would have allowed the researcher to determine whether this took place. Without a control group and a placebo group to provide a base line against which to compare the performance of the drug groups, it would be difficult for the researcher to draw any firm conclusions about the effects of the drug. It should be pointed out, however, that he would have some information because he did use three dosage levels in his study. If his analysis had shown that the subjects in the three-bennies group reacted significantly faster than those in the two-bennies group and that this group reacted faster than the subjects in the one-benny group, he might conclude that there was a drug effect. However, since he found no significant differences among these groups and since he had no groups of subjects who did not receive the drug, his results have little meaning.

The dependent variable selected for study is an example of a variable of convenience—in this case one that is not particularly relevant to the question being asked. Although reaction time is an important aspect of the entire driving task, much more is involved than just responding by means of a telegraph key to the onset of a red light. There are difficulties associated with defining "driver behavior" and with selecting relevant dependent variables, but there are many more meaningful measures that could have been used. Thus, he might have tested his subjects in a driving simulator or in an instrumented research vehicle. The point is that even if all the other features—random selection and assignment, manipulation of independent variables, and control of extraneous variables—had been carefully dealt with, using an irrelevant dependent variable resulted in a study of little value.

Some obvious extraneous variables would have to have been considered in this design. That the temperature was considerably higher for one experimental group than for the other two is one uncontrolled nuisance variable. We have already mentioned subject sex as an extraneous variable that could have been controlled by matching. Some other nuisance variables are less obvious. For example, the dosage of amphetamine given the subjects was one, two, or three pills. Would a subject who weighed 100 pounds respond to a given dosage in the same way that a 220-pound subject would? Some subjects were tested immediately after being given the drug, while others were tested some time later. A drug has a certain point after ingestion when it results in the greatest behavioral response. This may be about 30 minutes with amphetamine. The subjects tested immediately after receiving the drug may have shown no drug effect, while the effect may have worn off in those tested an hour or two after receiving the drug.

The reader can probably find several other design flaws. It should be obvious, however, from the shortcomings already discussed that this experiment did not answer the research question and thus must be considered a poor experiment. As we have indicated, this is an exaggerated example of a poor experiment, and it is unlikely that any researcher would conduct a study with a design as poor as this one. Often the design shortcomings of a study are not at all obvious, and it takes an expert to detect them. However, if the reader looks for the important features of the experimental methods we have discussed—control of intersubject differences, control of extraneous variables, appropriate dependent variables, and manipulation of independent variables—he will find studies that are weak in one or more of these areas.

The Field Experiment

In our discussion of the experimental method, we have used as examples studies conducted in laboratories. Often, however, the experimental method is used by researchers in nonlaboratory settings. These studies are called *field experiments*. They take place in many natural settings, such as automobiles, schools, factories, communities, and parks. The following is an example.

Case 4.5. A researcher is interested in the effects of alcohol on driver performance. He designs an instrumentation package for a car that will enable him to obtain a number of measures of driver performance, such as steering and speed control. He randomly assigns drivers to three conditions—a control group, a group with a blood-alcohol concentration (BAC) of .05, and a group with a BAC of .08. All the subjects drive the test vehicle over a 20-mile stretch of lightly traveled state highway.

This study shows that often the distinction between a laboratory experiment and a field experiment is not a sharp one. Although most investigators would consider this study a field experiment, others would argue that it qualifies as a laboratory experiment in the sense that the instrumented vehicle can be considered a traveling laboratory. Usually, however, the distinction is clearer. For example, much research is conducted in schools, where various methods of instruction are evaluated in actual classroom situations. Most of the research conducted on new training techniques in industry and the military can be considered field experiments.

In general, then, field experiments take place in realistic, natural settings where one or more independent variables are manipulated and conditions are controlled as carefully as possible. Although the researcher may lack *full* experimental control over all the variables, he can still exert considerable control. As Campbell and Stanley (1966) point out:

> There are many natural social settings in which the research person can introduce something like experimental design into his scheduling of data collection procedures (e.g., the *when* and *to whom* of measurement), even though he lacks the full control over the scheduling of experimental stimuli (the *when* and *to whom* of exposure and the ability to randomize exposures) which makes a true experiment possible. Collectively, such situations can be regarded as quasi-experimental designs [p. 34].

Much of the research discussed in the next chapter involves a *quasi-experimental design* as described by Campbell and Stanley.

Although the control of the variables in a field experiment is usually not as tight as in a laboratory experiment, the field experiment has several virtues that make it a useful method for the behavioral scientist. The realism of the research setting is one important advantage, as we shall see when we discuss the problem of the generalizability of laboratory findings. Realism in the research setting usually makes generalizations to other situations more valid.

Many kinds of behavior that are difficult to study in the laboratory experiment can be studied in the field experiment. For example, many questions that educators are interested in can be studied in the school but not in the laboratory. Certain kinds of complex social interactions and processes are also more effectively investigated in natural settings. In general, "Flexibility and applicability to a wide variety of problems are important characteristics of field experiments..." (Kerlinger, 1964, p. 385).

Simulation Studies

Though we have defined a field experiment as one that takes place in a natural setting, in some cases realistic settings are also employed in the laboratory study. In other words, a real world setting is *simulated* in the laboratory, and the investigator studies behavior in this setting.

A variety of types of real world settings can be and have been simulated in laboratories. Business and industrial settings are simulated and the decision-making behavior of executives studied. Social systems are simulated and such processes as communications, decision making, and leadership behavior investigated. Man-machine systems are simulated and the behavior of operators in these systems studied.

The reader is probably most familiar with the last type of simulation situation. Everyone who has watched the moon shots on television has been exposed to the elaborate simulators used to train the astronauts. Though simulators are often designed for training purposes, others have been constructed for research. For example, a driving simulator in the authors' laboratory has been used in a wide range of studies concerned with driver behavior. This is an elaborate simulator that is very realistic and allows the experimenter to obtain a number of measures of driver performance. Such a simulator is particularly useful in studies of the effects of alcohol and other drugs on driver behavior, since the "accidents" that the subjects have when driving the simulator do not result in physical injury. In fact, one of the major advantages of using a simulator instead of the real world setting is that studies can be conducted that are too dangerous to do in the real setting. A disadvantage of simulator research, however, is that it still only simulates and is not as realistic as the actual setting would probably be.

THE RELEVANCE OF LABORATORY STUDIES TO REAL WORLD PROBLEMS

We pointed out earlier that more and more researchers in the behavioral sciences are trying to answer questions that arise because of real world problems. In attempting to answer these questions, however, the investigators often use the experimental method in neatly controlled laboratory studies. A question that is beginning to be asked with increased frequency is "How relevant are the findings of these laboratory studies to the real world problems?"

In considering the laboratory experiment, it is important to keep in mind that it is at best only a rough model of the real world situation it is designed to represent. Chapanis (1967), in a thought-provoking article on the relevance of laboratory studies to practical situations, points out:

> . . . as representations of the real world, models are *always* incomplete and so are *always* wrong. It follows, therefore, that insofar as they try to represent or model the real world, laboratory experiments are always wrong, too. To put this another way, the results of laboratory experiments always fail to give us exact solutions to real-world problems. In some cases, to be sure, the results of a laboratory experiment may be substantially correct; that is, it may predict with reasonably good accuracy how people do indeed behave in life. At the other extreme, however, the results of laboratory experiments may not even come close to predicting human behavior. And, of course, one can get all possible gradations between these two extremes [pp. 561–562].

Perhaps the most critical factors limiting the generalizability of laboratory findings to the real world are associated with the selection and manipulation of the independent variables and the selection of the dependent variable.

The Independent Variables

We have already discussed how, in a typical experiment, there are numerous variables that may have an effect on the dependent variable. The experimenter usually selects a limited number of these variables to serve as his independent variables; some of the others (the extraneous variables) are controlled or held constant. Many are simply ignored. In the real life situation, however, many variables influence behavior, and they are not held constant, controlled, or, for that matter, ignored. They all influence the behavior of the individual. One of the primary reasons, then, that it is often hazardous to generalize from the laboratory to the real world is that the laboratory experiment involves a very limited number of independent variables, while the real world situation involves a virtually unlimited number.

Another problem is that the variables used in the laboratory may be different from those they are supposed to represent in the real world. Bringing a variable into the laboratory will change it in some ways. A variable in the real world contains a number of elements. When the researcher brings a variable into the laboratory, he is likely to lose some of its original elements (Chapanis, 1967, p. 566). For example, when we attempt to study the effects of stress in a laboratory setting, the type of stress that we can induce by electric shock or some other means is probably quite different from the stress involved in many real world situations.

Although in many situations an independent variable such as stress may lose something when it is brought into the laboratory, in other cases something may be added. For example, an important element added to the independent variable when it is brought into the laboratory is the experimenter himself. It has been demonstrated in a number of studies that the presence of the experimenter may modify the behavior of the subject; even when the experimenter is not physically present, the fact that the subject knows he is in an experiment may modify his behavior. Chapanis's point, that variables change when they are abstracted from real life situations and brought into the laboratory, is an important one that experimenters concerned with real world problems must constantly keep in mind.

Dependent Variables

We pointed out in discussing the experiment on the effects of amphetamine on driver performance that the dependent variable selected (reaction time) was not very relevant to driver performance. The task of the subject, pressing a key when a light went on, bears little resemblance to the real life situation in which an individual in an automobile must respond to external situations by braking, accelerating, swerving, or other ways.

All too often the dependent variables are variables of convenience in that they are selected because they are easy to measure. That they are often selected for convenience and may not be particularly relevant to the research question is another reason that it is often difficult to apply findings from laboratory experiments to real world problems.

Chapanis points out another methodological factor often characterizing the laboratory study that may reduce the generalizability of the findings. To obtain enough data from a subject, the experimenter may speed up the presentation of stimuli and in other ways tend to overload the subject in the laboratory study. Thus, in a study of reaction time in the laboratory, the subject may have to respond to the onset of a light every ten seconds for a 30-minute period. Obviously, a driver does not ordinarily have to respond this frequently. By speeding up the presentation of stimuli and by adding irrelevant and distracting tasks, the researcher makes the laboratory task much more difficult than the real world task that it is designed to represent. By deliberately distorting real life conditions for his experiment, the researcher again makes it difficult to translate his findings to the real life situation.

We have considered what many feel is a major limitation of the experimental method. However, in discussing the problem of applying the results of laboratory findings to the much more complex situations encountered in daily living, Arnoult (1972) makes an important point:

> There is no doubt that laboratory research involves artificial situations which are usually much simpler than the outside world, but this fact does not detract from the value of experimental research. Experiments in every science involve artificially simplified situations. Only in this way can a scientist hope to isolate the individual effects of the many variables that might be importantly related to the phenomenon under investigation. The relationships that are found are not intended to be applied without discretion to events in the everyday world. Scientific generalizations are intended to apply *in principle* to a wide range of phenomena but may not be an exact description of any real event [p. 52].

SUMMARY

Based on the amount of control that a researcher has over the experimental situation and the research variables involved, research methods can be classified as (1) the experimental method, in which the researcher can exert the most control; (2) the testing method, in which less control is possible; and (3) the systematic observation method, in which the researcher makes no attempt to manipulate or control the situation.

In designing an experiment, the researcher must pay particular attention to (1) the selection and measurement of the dependent variable, (2) the selection and assignment of subjects, (3) the selection and manipulation of independent variables, and (4) the control of nuisance variables.

Proper subject selection and assignment will assure the investigator that groups of subjects exposed to the experimental conditions are equivalent and that, if the groups behave differently under the experimental conditions, the differences are due to the conditions and not to intersubject differences existing before the experiment. Selection and assignment of subjects involve randomization whenever possible, with the subjects selected and assigned to groups at random and with the experimental treatment conditions assigned at random.

In the experimental method the independent variable is manipulated in such a fashion that the subjects are exposed to conditions representing two or more values of the variable. The investigator determines whether the dependent variable varies systematically with the values of the independent variable.

In some studies the effects of a single independent variable are determined. Usually, several independent variables are involved (a factorial design), in which case the investigator is concerned with not only the *main* effects of the independent variables but also *interaction* effects.

Variables other than the independent variables may have an effect on the behavior of interest. These are called extraneous or nuisance variables. The investigator must keep these types of variables from influencing his results, whether by holding these variables constant or by randomization.

An important purpose of research design is to control variance—that is, the variability of the measures obtained for the dependent variable. Three kinds of variance are of most concern in designing an experiment: experimental variance, extraneous variance, and error variance.

METHODS OF OBSERVING BEHAVIOR II: TESTING AND SYSTEMATIC OBSERVATION

5

In the experimental method the researcher manipulates independent variables and observes the effect of his manipulation on the dependent variable. Characteristic of the experimental method is the researcher's tight control over the independent variables.

The experimenter does not have this kind of control over the independent variables with the methods discussed in this chapter. Often the independent variable of interest is a *classificatory,* or *internal, variable,* such as age, sex, intelligence, educational background, or socioeconomic status. Research with independent variables of this kind is often referred to as *ex post facto research.* Kerlinger (1964) defines this as *"research in which the independent variable or variables have already occurred and in which the researcher starts with the observations of a dependent variable or variables. He then studies the independent variables in retrospect for their possible relations to, and effects on, the dependent variable or variables"* (p. 360).

The point to remember is that in ex post facto research, unlike experimental research, the investigator does not have control over his independent variables because they have already occurred. Moreover, the researcher using this method often cannot use randomization, which, as we pointed out in the previous chapter, is another form of control available to the investigator using the experimental method. These are built-in weaknesses, then, of ex post facto research. However, as we shall see in this chapter, this type of research also has advantages.

THE TESTING METHOD

The testing method, or "systematic assessment with controlled stimuli" (Scott & Wertheimer, 1962, p. 74), gives the behavioral scientist some control over the research variables but not to the extent possible with the experimental method. Thus, when data are obtained by testing, it is often difficult to say that variable X causes behavior Y because many extraneous variables that might also affect the behavior cannot be (or are not) controlled or held constant in the typical testing situation.

The behavioral scientist using the testing method is often investigating some characteristic of a group of individuals. To do so, he designs a standard stimulus situation that he assumes will elicit responses reflecting the characteristic. For example, the test that the reader takes in this course will probably consist of questions designed to elicit responses reflecting a particular characteristic—knowledge of the material covered. The reader may have taken other tests designed to assess general intelligence, ability to perform certain tasks, attitudes toward particular topics, and so forth. Interviews, questionnaires, and opinion surveys are also examples of tests used by behavioral scientists. No effort will be made here to discuss the wide variety of types of tests. They do have in common, however, a controlled stimulus situation designed to elicit responses revealing something about the individual involved.

An important difference between the testing method and the experimental method must be kept in mind. A test of some type can be, and often is, used as the measure of the dependent variable in an experimental study. In such cases the investigator manipulates one or more independent variables and measures the effects of this manipulation on some aspect of behavior with a test of some kind, such as an attitude test, an intelligence test, or a test of knowledge in a given area. In other investigations, however, a test is administered to a large group of individuals to assess similarities or differences among these individuals in a particular characteristic. No manipulation of independent variables is involved. For an illustration of the difference between a test used in an experiment and a test used as an assessment device, consider the following examples:

Case 5.1. The army was interested in determining the effectiveness of two new types of instruction in basic electronics over the method of instruction that had been used for a number of years. A total of 300 enlisted men, all qualified for electronics training, were randomly assigned to one of three groups, for a total of 100 per group. The three groups consisted of the standard instruction (control) group and two experimental groups, each receiving a different type of instruction. All the instructors were carefully trained to control instructor differences. At the end of the training program, which lasted one month, the students in each of the three groups were given an identical battery of tests designed to measure their knowledge of basic electronics. The results showed that the subjects in one of the experimental groups performed significantly better than the subjects in the standard instruction group, while the subjects in the other experimental group performed worse than the control subjects. It was decided to implement the experimental method of instruction that had proved to be superior to the standard instruction.

Case 5. 2. Since a great deal of work had gone into the development of the tests used in the above experiment, one of the administrators at the electronics school decided to do some further research using the tests. He was interested in assessing the knowledge of basic electronics that the soldiers had had before receiving any instruction in the school. Consequently, he established a procedure in which all new students were given the tests the day before they started school. After analyzing the data from several hundred subjects, the investigator had a good understanding of his students' knowledge of electronics before they entered the school. On the basis of this information, students were assigned to an accelerated or a regular class.

In the first case the basic electronics tests were used as a measure of the dependent variable (knowledge of electronics), and the effects of three methods of instruction (independent variables) on the dependent variable were determined. Thus, the experimental method was used. However, in the second case, although the tests were used to assess knowledge of basic electronics, there was no manipulation of independent variables. Rather, the tests assessed the degree to which a number of individuals possessed a particular attribute—in this instance a knowledge of basic electronics. This is an example of ex post facto research.

Survey Research

We are often bombarded with the results of one type of survey research—public opinion polling. The survey researcher attempts in some systematic fashion to obtain data from populations (or samples of populations) to assess some characteristics of the population. In the surveys conducted before elections, for example, the researchers attempt to assess the voting behavior of the population.

Although the survey technique is often considered to be a separate method of studying behavior, this technique can appropriately be discussed as a form of the testing method. In survey research the characteristic of interest is generally assessed by a test of some type, usually a structured interview. By means of the interview or another data-gathering device, the researcher attempts to determine the frequency of occurrence of, the distribution of, and the relationships among a variety of variables. Sometimes the interviews are designed to obtain *facts* about a population—the Census Bureau surveys, for example—but in most cases the object of a survey is to assess the *attitudes* and *opinions* of a population.

Although the researcher using the survey technique is typically interested in assessing the characteristics of entire populations, only on rare occasions can an entire population be studied. Consequently, survey researchers usually study samples drawn from populations and, from these, attempt to infer the attributes of the population. One of the most important elements of the survey technique is the method of sampling employed; the researcher must be certain that his sample is representative of the population. The sampling procedures used by survey researchers have been discussed in detail in a previous chapter and will not be considered here. It is important to remember, however, that improper sampling will negate the results of any survey. There are, of course, other important features of a survey approach. For example, the construction of the interview questions is very important—they must not only get at what the researcher is interested in but also forestall distortion or feigning of responses. Thorough training of the interviewers is also an important requirement of a good survey.

When a survey is properly conducted, its results are often surprisingly accurate. Usually, however, because of the amount of information that the surveyer attempts to obtain, his information is superficial.

The Case Study Approach

In some instances a behavioral scientist is interested in how a characteristic of an individual emerged and developed over time. For example, a clinical psychologist treating a neurotic patient would be interested in finding out how the neurotic symptoms first emerged and how they changed over time. To obtain this information, he would use the case study method. Through interviews the clinician would amass data on the life history of his patient that would result in a detailed biography. The clinician would, hopefully, have considerable information on the etiology and development of the neurosis by the end of his interview.

The case study method is one of the principal sources of data for the clinical psychologist, but it is also used by behavioral scientists in many fields. Although usually the case being studied is a single person, the method can be employed effectively in other situations. "The case study intensively examines many characteristics of one 'unit' (person, work group, company, community, culture), usually over a long period of time. The goal of such investigations is to learn 'all' about the area of interest for the one case involved" (Berelson & Steiner, 1964, p. 27).

Although we can get a great deal of information about a person, an industry, a community, a culture, and so forth with the case study method, the approach has limitations. Since only one unit is involved, the generalizability of the findings based on this method is unknown. It is, of course, ex post facto research, and the limitations of this type of research have been discussed earlier. On the other hand, the case study method is a particularly fruitful approach for generating ideas and insights and for suggesting hypotheses for research. It should be kept in mind, however, that this method merely generates insights and hypotheses; it does not test or demonstrate them.

In many respects the case study method is similar to the survey approach. Whereas the sample survey is used to measure a few characteristics of a large number of individuals, the case study method is used to examine numerous characteristics of one person or unit. An important difference, however, is that the sample survey usually measures these characteristics at one specific time, while the case study method is a study of long-time characteristics.

THE SYSTEMATIC OBSERVATION METHOD

Observation of behavior is, of course, a fundamental aspect of all the methods used to study behavior. In the experimental method the investigator observes the behavior of interest either directly or with instruments and determines what effect the manipulation of independent variables has on the behavior. Similarly, with the testing method the researcher observes his subjects' responses to standard stimulus situations. As we have pointed out, with the experimental method the observations of behavior take place under highly controlled and often artificial conditions. The testing method, which is not as controlled as the experimental method, relies to a great extent on what can be termed retrospective data—that is, information that must be recollected, which is often unreliable.

With the systematic observation method behavior can be studied as it occurs in an uncontrolled, natural setting, and the researcher need not depend on the subject's ability or willingness to respond verbally or otherwise to experimental variables or to a test of some kind. Rather, the researcher observes and records the behavior that occurs in a particular setting without intruding. He does not attempt to manipulate independent variables, nor does he usually try to control or eliminate extraneous variables.

The observation method has been used in a wide range of behavioral studies for a variety of different purposes:

> It may be used in an exploratory fashion, to gain insights that will later be tested by other techniques; its purpose may be to gather supplementary data that may qualify or help to interpret findings obtained by other techniques; or it may be used as the primary method of data collection in studies designed to provide accurate descriptions of situations or to test causal hypotheses [Selltiz, Jahoda, Deutsch, & Cook, 1962, p. 204].

Generally, a scientist uses the systematic observation technique when he wants to study behavior as it occurs in a natural setting, such as a school, a community, or a playground, where subjects are likely to demonstrate the relevant behavior. This method is thus frequently referred to as the *naturalistic observation method*. Sometimes, however, the subjects are in a laboratory, and their behavior is observed under other than natural conditions. If the researcher does not manipulate independent variables and observes and records the behavior as it occurs, he is still using the systematic observation method. On the other hand, some of the techniques used in this method can be used effectively in experimental studies in which independent variables are manipulated and the observational techniques are used to measure the dependent variable, the behavior of the organism. Thus, the terminology used in behavioral research literature is often confusing; an experimenter who actually used the experimental method and manipulated several independent variables may refer to his study as a systematic observation study simply because he used observational techniques to record the data for his dependent variable. Consider the following examples:

Case 5.3. In an effort to understand better the behavior of children as they cross streets and to determine what types of behavior might contribute to pedestrian accidents, Heimstra, Nichols, and Martin (1969) used the naturalistic observation method. On a street corner near a school that was regularly used by a large number of children, a concealed camera man filmed children as they approached and crossed the street. The motion pictures obtained were carefully studied by means of a single frame projection system and the behavior of the children analyzed individually. Information on each child was obtained on social conditions, interaction with other children, how rapidly the child approached the curb, whether he stopped at the curb, whether he watched for traffic when he stopped, and so on. The investigators concluded, among other things, that girls were more likely to stop at the curb and watch for traffic than were boys and that, in general, girls crossed the street in a much safer fashion than did boys.

Case 5.4. The same investigators (in an unpublished study) attempted to determine whether the street-crossing behavior of children could be modified. Using the technique described above, they observed kindergarten children from three different schools crossing the street. The observations were recorded for a number of days, and the frequency of certain types of high-risk behavior was obtained. The two types of high-risk behavior of most interest were not stopping at the curb and stopping but not watching for traffic. After the initial period of observations, the students in one school were given a series of lectures on proper street crossing, and the students in the second school were shown a series of films on street-crossing behavior; the students in the third school served as control subjects and received no special training. At the end of a three-week period, another series of observations was made and the frequency of the high-risk kinds of behavior compared with the frequency during the first series of observations. The researchers found that there was no difference in frequency for students in the control group but that there was a reduction in frequency in the two experimental groups.

Although the same techniques were used for observing and recording behavior in this study as were used in the first study as well as the same natural setting, there is an important difference. In the second study the experimental method was employed, since an independent variable (safety training) was manipulated and the effects of this manipulation on a dependent variable (street-crossing behavior) determined. Thus, even though observational techniques were used, it was an experiment. In the remainder of our discussion on the systematic observation method, we will be concerned with its use in studying behavior occurring in a natural setting where the observer does not manipulate independent variables.

The purposes of the study, the location of the subjects, the types of subjects, and other considerations will determine the particular techniques selected by the researcher in conducting a naturalistic observation study. However, several broad methodological decisions confront any investigator wishing to use this approach. He must carefully consider and decide on the setting for the study, the behavior to be observed, and the way in which he will record his observations. Although there are other important considerations, we will focus on the above in our discussion.

The Setting for the Study

Any location in which the behavior of interest occurs can be considered to qualify for the observational setting. Usually the setting is determined by the objectives of the study. Thus, an anthropologist studying the aggressive behavior of baboons makes his observations in a setting quite different from that used by a psychologist interested in the social behavior of nursery school children. Both, however, study their subjects in a natural setting.

If the setting is determined by the objectives of the study, why is this an important consideration for the researcher? In many instances the decision is not important, for the study can be conducted effectively in the natural setting. A problem arises, however, in cases in which the natural setting has certain characteristics that may interfere with clear observations. In these situations the investigator must decide whether to modify the setting in some way.

Some researchers argue that any modification of the natural setting will destroy the meaningfulness of the data obtained. They feel that if changes in the setting are required in order to use the observational method, it should not be used. Other researchers, however, argue that *subtle* modifications of the setting are not only permissible but, in many instances, desirable. Usually the observer is concerned with a selected range of behavior, so that portions of the natural setting irrelevant to that behavior can be modified with no or minimal effects on it. If some modification of the setting would enhance the researcher's ability to observe the behavior he is concerned with, most investigators would not hesitate to make the modification. For example, a researcher studying the social behavior of nursery school children may wish to identify the children in some fashion—perhaps by having them wear different color jackets. Such a modification is unlikely to have any effect on the behavior. He could probably make numerous other minor changes as well. However, as Weick (1968) notes, "Subtlety in modifications, however, is a question of degree and it can plausibly be argued that subtlety is no guarantee that naturalness is preserved" (p. 367). The concern of the investigator, then, is to preserve the naturalness of the setting when he makes modifications. Yet modifications may not be as disruptive as many investigators think. Weick adds:

> Perhaps the most significant force that counteracts the disruptive effect of modifications is the fact that persons are operating in settings that are familiar. They are apt to be preoccupied with everyday events, and any slight changes in this routine are apt to be assimilated and to attract little attention [p. 368].

The Observer in the Setting. Although minor modifications of the setting probably will not have a disruptive effect, one important modification is the presence of the observer himself. In many studies the subjects know that the observer is present; and even if they accept his presence and take it for granted, it may have some impact on their behavior.

The relationship between the observer and those being observed can vary considerably depending on the study. The observer may actively participate as a member of the group he is observing, he may be considered a member of the group but not actively participate, or he may be an observer who is not part of the group. The members of the group may or may not know that they are being observed. When they do know, the observer must ask himself how much this knowledge will interfere with the naturalness of the situation and the behavior he is observing.

Possibly the best way to deal with the interference problem is *concealing* the observer and disguising that observations are being made. Thus, in the studies of street-crossing behavior mentioned earlier, the children were filmed by a concealed cameraman and did not know that they were being observed. In this case the observer was actually hidden from view. However, in any situation where the group under observation is unaware that it is being observed, the concealment strategy is involved.

Earlier in the text the question of ethics in experimentation was discussed in some detail. Obviously, whenever a researcher observes a group without its knowledge, the question of ethics arises, particularly when the behavior of interest is behavior normally not open to public scrutiny. The investigator must be certain that the potential findings of his study are important enough to justify concealment.

What to Observe

The question of what kinds of behavior to observe will be answered in part by the objectives of the study. However, the researcher must overcome his impulse to attempt to observe, record, and analyze all the behavior—both verbal and nonverbal—that may occur in a given situation, since doing so is difficult or impossible. Rather, he must select the kind or kinds of behavior of most interest and concentrate on these.

Because the range of behavior that can be studied with the naturalistic observation technique is so extensive, we will attempt only to list some general categories of behavior commonly studied in human subjects. Obviously, when various species of lower animals are studied by this method, the kinds of behavior will vary considerably.

Weick (1968) classifies the kinds of behavior for observation as (1) nonverbal behavior, (2) spatial behavior, (3) extralinguistic behavior, and (4) linguistic behavior. In a particular study the observer might concentrate on one, two, or even all of these categories.

Nonverbal Behavior.   This type of behavior consists of bodily movements, including gestures, facial expressions, and exchanged glances. Each of these kinds of nonverbal behavior has been extensively studied and has been found to be correlated with important psychological processes. It has been shown, for example, that the characteristics and frequency of each type will differ considerably depending on the situation.

Spatial Behavior.   As Weick (1968) points out:

> People are active. They mill, move towards, move away from, linger, wander, dart, maintain closeness, maintain distance, or show any one of a number of attempts to structure the space around them. The frequency and range of these movements as well as their outcomes (for example, cliques) are easily observed . . . [pp. 388–389].

Although human spatial behavior has not been studied very often in the past, our knowledge of it is increasing. For example, territoriality, a form of spatial behavior that has been demonstrated in numerous species of animals, is now being studied in humans. Analysis of spatial behavior in groups may reveal a great deal about the structure of the groups and about the quality and content of the relationships among the members.

Extralinguistic Behavior.   "When a person says something, the words or linguistic content actually constitute a relatively small portion of the verbal behavior which the alert observer can record" (Weick, 1968,

p. 391). The manner in which a person speaks may supply important data to the observer. For example, the pitch, loudness, and timbre of the voice may reflect the individual's affective state. His rate of speaking, whether he interrupts, and other characteristics of his speech may furnish the observer with clues to the psychological state of the speaker. If the researcher can observe and record these kinds of noncontent speech behavior, he may obtain considerably more information about his subjects than he would if he simply records what they have to say.

Linguistic Behavior. One of the most common forms of behavior recorded in naturalistic observation studies is talk. There are a variety of ways in which the observer can record what is said and several methods by which he can analyze it. These methods are too complex to consider here, but, basically, all are designed to evaluate the interactions of the speakers with others in both quantitative and qualitative characteristics. In other words, these methods examine not only how often a person spoke but whether he was being assertive, antagonistic, anxious, and so forth when he did so.

Recording the Observations

There are numerous techniques for recording observations. These techniques range all the way from a pencil and notepad to highly sophisticated and elaborate instrument systems. Motion picture systems are common, tape recorders may be used by the researcher who orally records his observations, and videotape systems are frequently used, as are a variety of other devices. But regardless of the specific recording system used, the important consideration is that the data recorded can later be summarized and analyzed.

Typically, the summary and analysis of the data involve breaking down the observed behavior into a number of rather narrow behavioral categories. The categories used will depend to a great extent on the objective of the study. Thus, a study of aggressive behavior in children may need a number of categories representing different types of aggressive behavior and only a few broad categories encompassing the other types of behavior observed.

Often, through preliminary observation of the behavior of interest, the researcher defines a number of behavior categories before he begins his observations and then records only the behavior fitting these categories.Thus, the researcher studying aggressive behavior in children might record only the instances of aggressive behavior that occurred and ignore the other types of behavior.

One of the important purposes of categorizing the behavior is that it allows the observational data to be quantified. Although observation of behavior can be valuable to the researcher in providing insights and developing hypotheses, his observations must be quantified in some fashion if he is to test any hypotheses by means of the observational method. Quantification may involve simply counting the incidences of behavior recorded in a particular category, or it may involve rather elaborate analyses, as is the case when attempts are made to predict the probability of occurrence of one type of behavior from the preceding behavior.

Reliability of the System

Because the observational method depends to a great extent on subjective judgments of the observers, the question of reliability is critical. When an observer is recording what he considers to be aggressive behavioral events among a group of children, he is making a subjective judgment even though he may have carefully defined his categories of aggressive behavior.

The reliability of the observational method can be increased in several ways. One way is to define each category in such a fashion that it is difficult to record any behavior other than the behavior fitting the definition. Certain types of recording systems are more reliable than others, so, if possible, the observer should select one of these. Finally, the researcher should know the reliability of his system. One common way to assess reliability when using the observational method is by means of co-observers. In this method two observers record the behavior of interest independently and then compare, usually by correlation, their observations. If there is a high positive correlation between the two sets of observations, the system is usually assumed to be reliable.

A COMPARISON OF THE METHODS

At the beginning of this chapter, we pointed out that one way to classify research methods is on the basis of the amount of control that the investigator has over the research variables. On this basis the experimental method offers the most control, the testing method less control, and the observational method the least control. In discussing the experimental method, we considered several means for maintaining control. Three of these are the *hold constant* approach, *randomization*, and *systematic variation*.

These strategies of control can be used to a lesser extent in the testing and observational methods. For example, in both of these methods, certain aspects of the situation in which the behavior is studied can be held constant. Thus, an interviewer might always conduct his interviews in his home or his office and at the same time of day. The researcher using the observational method might also record his observations at a given time of the day, in certain kinds of weather, and at the same location. The interviewer will probably hold his interview technique and format constant, while the observer will use a standard observation and recording technique. Randomization and systematic variation can also be used to a limited extent in the testing and observational approaches to control extraneous variables. However, in control of extraneous variables, the observational method has *slight* control, the testing method *some* control, and the experimental method *much* control.

As Scott and Wertheimer (1962) point out, control is not the only factor that must be considered in designing a research project. They discuss the three methods in terms of the criteria of *precision, repeatability,* and *generalizability.*

A precise research design is one that "permits accurate measurement of the variables under study and specified statements concerning their functional interrelations" (p. 94). According to this criterion we must again rate the experimental method first, since precise measurement is possible and functional relationships can be established by manipulating the independent variables. With the testing method retrospective data are obtained, which may or may not correspond to the real facts. Similarly, in observational studies precise measurement of the dependent variables may be difficult. In neither of these methods is it possible to manipulate independent variables to establish causal relationships.

Repeatability, the second characteristic of a good research design, means that the procedures involved in a study can be easily duplicated by another investigator who wishes to see whether he will obtain the same results. Although it is often easier to repeat a study that used the experimental method, the three approaches are "potentially subject to comparable degrees of repeatability, given adequate sampling and stability in the phenomenon under study" (p. 95). Thus, the methods can be considered about equivalent in repeatability.

We have already discussed in some detail the problem of generalizing laboratory findings to the real world. Frequently the generalizability of results obtained with the testing method can also be questioned. Just because a person responds in a given fashion in a test situation, such as an interview, does not necessarily mean that he will actually behave in the manner indicated. Both the experimental method and the testing method usually involve responses elicited by the procedures used, so that data obtained with these methods may be less generalizable than those obtained with the observational method. It would appear that the systematic observation approach, if properly used, has a clear edge on the other methods in generalizability of findings to other situations.

COMBINING THE METHODS

As we indicated earlier, attempting to classify research designs as falling within the experimental method, the testing method, or the systematic observation method is, at best, arbitrary. Many research designs do not clearly fit any one of the strategies. Frequently a design combines features of two or even all three of the methods.

Case 5.5. A researcher was interested in evaluating the effects of a new drug thought to be effective in reducing anxiety. As a first step, he administered a test to a large number of potential subjects whose names had been drawn at random from those of all the students enrolled at a large university. The test was designed to reveal whether a person could be classified as high or low in anxiety. The researcher selected a number of subjects whose scores indicated that they were highly anxious and randomly assigned them to one of four groups. The subjects in one group were simply asked to report back to the laboratory each evening, while the subjects in the other three groups were asked to report to the student health center each morning for a one-week period and to report to the laboratory each evening. At the health center the subjects in one of the groups were given a coated sugar pill (placebo), the subjects in another group were given one dosage level of the new drug, and the subjects in the final group were given a second dosage level of the drug. The subjects did not know whether they received the drug or the placebo.

When the subjects reported back to the laboratory each night, they were placed for 30 minutes (as groups) in lounges with one-way mirrors and their behavior observed by concealed observers who had been thoroughly trained. The observers did not know what groups of subjects they were observing. The subjects were under the impression that the purpose of the half-hour meeting was to discuss a topic that was assigned before each session. A number of kinds of behavior that in earlier research had been shown to indicate anxiety were recorded. On the last evening all the subjects were again given the anxiety test. The test scorer did not know to what groups the subjects belonged.

Analysis of the test data revealed that the subjects in the high dosage level scored significantly lower on the anxiety test the second time they took it. The differences between scores on the pre-test and the post-test for subjects in the other groups were not significant. Analysis of the observational data revealed that the subjects in the high dosage group engaged in significantly less anxious behavior than did the subjects in the other groups during the last two observation sessions.

This study is an example of an investigation combining features of each of the methods discussed in this chapter. An independent variable (drug condition) was manipulated, and the effects of this manipulation on a dependent variable (performance as measured by the test and behavior as measured by systematic observation) were assessed. Thus, the experimental method was involved. The testing method was used to classify the subjects as highly anxious as well as to assess the effects of the drug. However, that the test showed a decrease in anxiety in the high dosage group would not necessarily mean that behavior associated with an anxious state would also be modified. The use of the observational technique, however, did reveal that this was the case.

This study includes several design features that were discussed briefly earlier but are worth brief mention again. The reader may have wondered why one group of anxious subjects received neither a placebo nor a drug but simply took the tests and reported to the laboratory. This group served as a second control group; the placebo group was the other. Sometimes in drug studies just the fact that the subjects have been given a placebo modifies their behavior to a considerable degree. This is called a *placebo effect*. In our example, if the placebo group, together with the drug groups, had shown a decrease in anxiety on the various measures but the other control group had not, what sort of interpretation would we put on the findings?

The subjects did not know whether they were receiving a placebo or a drug, nor did they know the purpose of the experiment. Keeping a subject in a drug study from knowing whether he received the drug is called the *single blind technique*. However, in this study the observers and the test scorer also did not know to what groups the subjects belonged. This technique is called a *double blind*. The double blind method is desirable in drug studies because it eliminates not only the possibility of a subject's behaving in a particular way just because he knows he has received a drug but also any bias on the part of the researchers, who may read things into their observations or scoring because they think a subject under a particular drug should behave in a certain way.

There are many other examples of *mixed models* of research. Often the researcher might be able to answer the question he is interested in by one of the methods but combines them for practical reasons (finances, availability of subjects, availability of facilities, and so on) or because he feels a mixed design will give him results in which he will have more confidence. Sometimes, however, a research project is so large that it is necessary to use all the methods to answer the research question. This is often the case in a type of research that is becoming increasingly common: *evaluative* or *impact* research.

Evaluative Research

The government annually spends many millions of dollars for various types of "action" programs designed to modify behavior in one way or another. There are programs to give underprivileged children special training, programs to reduce mental health problems, programs to reduce drug and alcohol problems, programs to train better drivers, and on and on.

At one time the granting agencies tended to be satisfied with a program if it appeared to be doing the job it was designed to do. However, in recent years they have taken a different view; most agencies now require proof that a program designed to change behavior actually does what it set out to do. This demand has resulted in evaluative research, which often does not neatly fit any of the models we have discussed. Since it has become so important, however, we will consider some of the key aspects of this kind of research.

We assume that action programs have specific objectives and that the purpose of evaluative research is to determine whether these objectives have been met. Although this seems like a reasonably straightforward statement, it is extremely difficult to make a clear statement of the objectives of many current programs. However, for evaluative research to be productive, the objectives of the program to be evaluated must be clearly stated. Beginning an evaluative research project without a definition of the objectives would be similar to starting an experiment without a statement of the research question to be answered.

Because action programs are designed to bring about changes in behavior, evaluative research can be thought of as a study of change. Although the methods used by the researcher to study the change may be complex, we can think of the basic strategy in rather simple terms:

> . . . the program to be evaluated constitutes the stimulus or "causal" or independent variable, while the desired change is similar to the "effect" or dependent variable. Characterized this way, one may formulate an evaluation project in terms of a series of hypotheses which state that "Activities *A, B,* and *C* will produce results *X, Y,* and *Z.*" Note that this formulation requires both a statement of the end result, or objectives of the program, *and* the specification of what it is about the program that might be expected to produce these results [Suchman, 1967, p. 38].

Although the basic strategy of evaluative research can be stated in simple terms, an actual evaluation project is usually complicated (and expensive) and presents the researcher with some unique problems that he normally does not encounter when employing the research methods discussed earlier in this chapter.

The evaluation research project is designed with the objectives of the action program in mind. The investigator takes into consideration the nature of the objectives (*what* kinds of behavior the action program is aimed at changing); whether the objectives are *unitary* or *multiple* (in that a single change or a series of changes may be the goal); the desired *magnitude* of the change; *when* the desired change is to take place; *who* the target of the program is (the groups or populations the program is aimed at); and *how* the objectives are to be gained. These questions are crucial to the design of the project, and the answers determine the methodological procedures—sampling, controls, measuring instruments, and analysis of the data.

Because evaluative research is aimed at measuring change, it is typically long-term research that lasts for the duration of an action program and, in many cases, even longer. Ideally, the evaluator works with the project director of the action program for some time before the program is implemented. This approach not only permits some design input from the evaluator that will increase the effectiveness of the evaluation project but also allows the evaluation team to gather some base-line data before the action program begins. Although this approach may seem the obvious one to use, in all too many instances evaluation is requested by some agency after an action program has been implemented or, sometimes, after it has been completed. In these situations evaluation research can yield little information about the changes accomplished by the action program. Currently, however, an evaluation phase is written into nearly all contracts or grants for action programs.

SUMMARY

When employing the testing method, the researcher uses a standard stimulus situation that will elicit responses from his subjects. These responses reflect some characteristic of interest. Tests are available that are designed to measure virtually all human attributes.

Survey research and case studies can be thought of as special examples of the testing method. Survey research methods are used to determine the frequency of occurrence, the distribution, and the relationships among a variety of variables. The case study method is used to examine intensively many characteristics of one unit over long periods. The unit may be a person, a group of persons, a company, and so forth.

With the systematic observation technique behavior can be studied as it occurs in a natural, uncontrolled setting. In designing a study using this technique, the investigator must be particularly concerned about (1) the setting for the study, (2) the behavior to be observed, and (3) the way in which he will record his observations.

The settings for observational studies vary considerably. In some cases the observer may have to modify the setting to some extent. If he does so, he must consider the effects of the modification on the observed behavior. Of particular importance is the possible effect of the observer's presence on the behavior.

A variety of types of behavior can be observed and recorded with the systematic observation method. Included are (1) nonverbal behavior, (2) spatial behavior, (3) extralinguistic behavior, and (4) linguistic behavior.

Observations are recorded in different ways. Of particular concern to the investigator is the reliability of the recording system he has developed. An important part of any observational study is the assessment of the reliability of the system.

Some research designs cannot be neatly categorized as experimental, testing, or systematic observation. Often a design combines features of all these methods. There are many examples of these mixed models of research.

6

THE ANALYSIS
OF RESEARCH
RESULTS

We have discussed a number of aspects of conducting various types of behavioral studies. In this chapter we will discuss several analytic methods that will finally enable us to provide answers to the questions initially prompting us to engage in the research process. These analytic methods are part of the area of inferential statistics known as hypothesis testing. In hypothesis testing we are concerned with the problem of inferring characteristics of a population from data collected from samples of that population. Through the appropriate application of statistical hypothesis tests, the researcher can evaluate the truth or falsity of specific statements, or hypotheses, about behavioral processes.

SCIENTIFIC VERSUS STATISTICAL HYPOTHESES

At the outset we must distinguish between two types of hypotheses involved in the research process. One type is the *scientific hypothesis*, which ordinarily is a relatively general statement of the question to which the research is addressed. An example is the following statement:

Alcohol intoxication will produce impairment of human decision-making processes.

This scientific hypothesis is the affirmative statement of a question we might wish to answer by conducting a behavioral experiment. The scientific hypothesis states the general nature of the relationship we expect to observe in the study. This hypothesis is not, however, directly testable in the form of a scientific hypothesis because it is a general statement whose terms need definition. We must, for example, provide an adequate definition of "alcohol intoxication" before we can assess the effects of this variable. Similarly, we must define a measure of "human decision making" to determine whether it is affected by alcohol intoxication. The step between the statement of the scientific hypothesis and the formulation of an explicit and testable statistical hypothesis involves the empirical definition of all these terms and the statement of the conditions of the experiment that will allow an evaluation of the relationship hypothesized. It is at this point that the careful definition of dependent and independent variables, selection and assignment of subjects, and careful experimental design enter.

The other type of hypothesis, the *statistical hypothesis,* is specific to the conditions of a particular study and is stated in such a form that it provides the direct basis for a statistical estimation of the degree to which generalizations can be made on the basis of the observations collected in the study. Meaningful statistical hypotheses are more specific statements of the relationships or experimental effects hypothesized, and they are usually phrased in terms of particular parameters or characteristics of the population of interest. A statistical hypothesis based on the scientific hypothesis introduced above might read as follows:

H_1:   Adult male subjects with a blood-alcohol concentration of .10 percent will exhibit a significantly increased mean response time to a three-choice reaction time task than will this population of individuals under a BAC condition of 0 percent.

Note that the statistical hypothesis mentions neither "alcohol intoxication" nor "decision-making processes." Instead of these hypothetical constructs used in the scientific hypothesis, the statistical hypothesis defines these variables in terms of the empirical conditions of the proposed experiment. In place of "alcohol intoxication," the statistical hypothesis defines a particular condition of the subjects, "a blood-alcohol concentration of .10 percent"; and instead of "decision-making processes," the statistical hypothesis specifies a performance measure and a testing situation, "response time to a three-choice reaction time task." Note also that the statistical hypothesis refers to the population of "adult males" and that the effect predicted by the statistical hypothesis involves a parameter of the distribution of choice reaction times of this population, the mean reaction time. A *population parameter* is the expected value of a particular statistical index based on the distribution of a given measure for the entire population. Population parameters are estimated from the data collected when observations are made of samples from a given population, and the inferential hypothesis-testing process involves estimating the degree to which observed differences between treatments in our sample can be generalized to the relevant population. In the case of the scientific and statistical hypotheses stated above, we are interested in determining whether we can conclude that a BAC level of .10 percent does, in general, increase mean reaction time of a choice reaction time task on the basis of differences in mean reaction time that we observe after testing a sample of individuals at the .10 percent BAC and again at the 0 percent BAC. In statistical terms our hypothesis is suggesting that the mean reaction time under a .10 percent BAC is representative of a different distribution of reaction times than is the mean reaction time under a 0 percent BAC condition. Statistical hypothesis tests can be applied to the data we obtain in this study to estimate the degree to which this statement can be accepted.

Alternative and Null Hypotheses

The form of statistical hypothesis stated above is referred to technically as the *alternative hypothesis*. The alternative hypothesis for a particular study follows directly from the scientific hypothesis and is generally a positive statement of the type of effect or relationship predicted in an experiment. The alternative hypothesis is not, however, the form of statistical hypothesis that is directly evaluated by a statistical test. The specific proposition tested by the inferential methods of hypothesis testing is the null hypothesis. The null hypothesis is the complement of the alternative hypothesis, or a hypothesis of no effect. In our example the null hypothesis might state:

H_0:   The mean choice reaction times of adult males tested under .10 percent and 0 percent BAC conditions are equal.

Note that the null hypothesis refers to a parameter of the population, as does its complement, the alternative hypothesis. This, however, is the proposition whose truth or falsity is estimated by the process of hypothesis testing. H_0 is used to refer to the null hypothesis, and H_1 represents the alternative hypothesis.

The hypothesis-testing process involves the collection of statistical evidence that forms the basis of a simple binary (two-choice) decision—to reject the null hypothesis or to fail to reject the null hypothesis. In the first case (rejection of the null hypothesis), support is implied for the alternative hypothesis. Thus, if the statistical evidence indicates rejection of the null hypothesis, we can at least tentatively accept the alternative hypothesis. Failure to reject the null hypothesis does not, however, mean the same thing as accepting the null hypothesis. If the evidence produced by the statistical test does not support rejection of the null hypothesis, we must conclude that we cannot accept the alternative hypothesis as stated, but we cannot ordinarily assume that this is adequate proof of the validity of the null hypothesis. The precise statistical logic leading to this type of statistical decision making is beyond the scope of this book. Suffice it to say that in science we do not prove hypotheses but systematically attempt to rule out alternative explanations. Thus, if statistical evidence from a hypothesis test leads us to reject a null hypothesis, we can rule out the null hypothesis and increase our confidence in the tenability of the alternative hypothesis, although we have not really proved the alternative hypothesis to be true. Conversely, if we fail to reject the null hypothesis, we can dismiss the alternative hypothesis we have stated, but we have not proved the null hypothesis to be true.

The decision-making process involved in hypothesis testing can be described in terms of the *decision matrix* shown in Table 6.1. The cells of this matrix indicate the four possible outcomes associated with the experimenter's decision on acceptance or rejection of the null hypothesis. The columns in this table represent the two possible true conditions of the population with respect to the hypothesis, while the rows represent the two possible statistically based decisions of the experimenter.

As indicated in this table, there are two ways in which the experimenter can be correct in deciding about the validity of his hypothesis and two ways in which he can be wrong. On the one hand, if the experimenter decides to reject the null hypothesis when the alternative hypothesis is true, he has made a correct decision. This outcome is shown in the upper left-hand cell of the table. The researcher is also correct, however, if he decides not to reject H_0 when H_1 is actually false (the lower right-hand cell of the table).

On the other hand, if the experimenter decides to reject H_0 when the alternative hypothesis is not a true statement, he will commit a Type I error. Conversely, if he fails to reject the null hypothesis when the alternative hypothesis is true, he commits a Type II error. Before considering the steps that are normally taken to minimize the chances of

TABLE 6.1.   The decision matrix for the hypothesis-testing decision. Rejecting the null hypothesis when it is false is a correct decision, while rejecting it when it is true results in a Type I error. Accepting H_0 when it is false leads to a Type II error, while accepting H_0 when it is true is another correct decision.

		True Condition in the Population	
		H_0 *False*	H_0 *True*
Decision	*Reject H_0*	Correct Decision Probability $= 1 - \beta$	Type I Error Probability $= \alpha$
	Accept H_0	Type II Error Probability $= \beta$	Correct Decision Probability $= 1 - \alpha$

committing Type I or Type II errors, let us briefly consider the implications of these distinct kinds of incorrect decisions.

The commission of a Type I error involves the acceptance as true of a false alternative hypothesis. Ordinarily the researcher is more sensitive to this type of error than he is to its converse, a Type II error. The seriousness of making this type of error, however, depends on the application that will be made of the results of a particular study. If, for example, we are conducting a study to determine whether drug X will immunize subjects against the plague, we can be justifiably hesitant to commit a Type I error, particularly if on the basis of our study the drug will be dispensed to people. In this case commission of a Type I error indicates that the alternative hypothesis is erroneous, that drug X may not provide the predicted immunity and people may die of the plague as a result. In a situation like this, it is much more appropriate to commit a Type II error, which would erroneously lead us to recommend not using the drug, than it would be to chance killing people as an indirect result of committing a Type I error. In most of the routine research of the behavioral scientist, however, we do not encounter situations as dramatic as this one, and a more likely risk associated with Type I errors is in wasting time believing in a false hypothesis and suffering the ridicule of one's colleagues for defending the false hypothesis.

The dread of committing a Type I error is firmly ingrained in many behavioral scientists, however, and is occasionally the cause of an unfortunate situation in behavioral research. Ordinarily, to reduce the probability of a Type I error, it is necessary to allow a greater chance of a Type II error. As a consequence, behavioral researchers may not detect experimental effects that may be important.

Significance Levels and Power

As we have indicated, in most tests of hypotheses the experimenter decides on an acceptable probability of a Type I error. This involves selecting a *significance level* for the statistical test of the hypothesis. This significance level, indicated by the Greek letter α, is the probability of occurrence of a Type I error. Perhaps the most widely used significance level in behavioral research is the .05 level. This indicates that, on the basis of the particular hypothesis test applied, the researcher will not reject the null hypothesis in favor of the alternative hypothesis unless, on the average, he can be assured of being correct 95 times out of 100, or, conversely, of being wrong only five out of 100 times. Again, it should be emphasized that this probability statement refers to the occurrence of a Type I error.

The probability of committing a Type II error in a hypothesis-testing situation is symbolized by the Greek letter β, and the term $1 - \beta$ is referred to as the *power* of the test. In this case "power" refers to the ability of the test to indicate rejection of the null hypothesis when the alternative hypothesis is true. Only rarely do we find cases in which the power of a hypothesis test, or the magnitude of β, is actually calculated, since this requires more information about the population than is ordinarily available to the researcher on the basis of his sample. We do know, however, that the power of a statistical hypothesis test is influenced by a number of factors, including both sample size and the size of α. Maximum power, and consequently minimum probability of a Type II error, is gained by increasing either the size of the sample or the probability of a Type I error.

Choosing a Statistical Test

For virtually any type of research design, a large number of hypothesis test models is available to assist the researcher in making his statistical decision on acceptance or rejection of the statistical hypothesis and the consequent acceptance or rejection of the scientific hypothesis on which H_1 is based. Perhaps one of the biggest problems of statistical inference facing the researcher is the selection of one statistical test from among so many plausible alternatives. One of the primary considerations in this choice relates to the type of measurement reflected in the data of a given study, or the scale of measurement on which the data are based. Recall from Chapter 2 that the amount of information contained in a particular score will depend on the scale of measurement on which the score is based and that different mathematical operations are appropriate with different scales of measurement. In particular, recall that nominal and ordinal scale measures are much less rigorous in the sense of the information that scores based on these scales contain than interval or ratio scale measures.

Two major varieties of statistical hypothesis tests are available to the researcher. His choice depends on the scale of measurement reflected in his data and the type of question he is attempting to answer. *Nonparametric* hypothesis tests are designed for use with nominal or ordinal scale data, although they can also be appropriately applied to interval or ratio data. *Parametric* tests are generally more appropriate for data representing measurement on at least an interval scale.

In the remainder of this chapter, we will discuss examples of both parametric and nonparametric hypothesis tests. This coverage is not intended to be exhaustive, however; the tests discussed are only representative of frequently used statistical tests. A great many additional hypothesis-testing models are available to the researcher, and a comprehensive review of all of them could fill several textbooks.

NONPARAMETRIC HYPOTHESIS TESTS

As we have indicated, nonparametric tests are designed for the statistical evaluation of hypotheses based on nominal or ordinal scale data. These tests can also be used with interval and ratio scale data and are particularly appropriate for these types of data if the assumptions required by parametric hypothesis tests cannot be met. Parametric tests frequently assume, for example, that the observations made in a given study are drawn from populations with specified shaped distributions of scores; nonparametric (or, more correctly, *distribution-free*) statistical tests do not depend on this assumption. To the extent that such assumptions cannot be met, the power (ability to reject correctly the null hypothesis) of parametric tests is affected. In such cases, even if our data represent interval scale measurement, nonparametric tests *may* be more appropriate than parametric tests in the evaluation of statistical hypotheses.

An additional advantage of nonparametric over parametric hypothesis tests, and one that will hopefully not have a bearing on the researcher's choice of tests, is that the nonparametric tests are usually much simpler to compute and do not require as many arithmetic and algebraic operations as the parametric tests. The reason for the mathematical simplicity of the nonparametric tests is simply that most arithmetic operations, except counting and ranking, are not meaningful with nominal and ordinal scale data. To illustrate nonparametric statistical methods, we will briefly discuss three of the most widely used of these techniques. Again, however, remember that these three techniques by no means exhaust the list of available nonparametric methods. For a description of other nonparametric techniques, the reader may wish to refer to Siegel (1956).

The χ^2 Single Sample Test

The χ^2 *single sample test* is an extremely important statistical method that can be appropriately applied to tests of hypotheses involving single samples of frequency count (nominal scale) data. Behavioral scientists frequently wish to test hypotheses related to the way in which individuals are distributed, according to a particular measure, in a population. Assume, for example, that we are conducting a study for the local police department to determine the number of drunks driving motor vehicles at different times during a particular nine-hour shift. The results of this study will be used to establish traffic law enforcement priorities for the department. If the overall time period in which we are interested extends from 7 PM to 4 AM, we might divide this nine-hour shift into three three-hour categories: 7 PM–10 PM, 10 PM–1 AM, and 1 AM–4 AM. We might then conduct a roadside survey in which we would randomly stop drivers and determine whether they are drunk (through a breath test, for example). The raw data for our study would then be the frequency count of drunk drivers during each of the three time periods. On the basis of this survey, we might obtain data similar to those shown in Table 6.2.

TABLE 6.2. Hypothetical data for χ^2 single sample test: number of drunk drivers by time period.

Time Period	Number of Drunks
7 PM - 10 PM	13
10 PM - 1 AM	33
1 AM - 4 AM	53

The alternative hypothesis that we wish to evaluate in this study can be stated as follows:

H_1:   The number of drunk drivers is not uniformly distributed among the three time periods (7-10, 10-1, and 1-4).

This, in turn, will specify the null hypothesis, which will be tested with the χ^2 single sample test:

H_0:   The number of drunk drivers is uniformly distributed across time periods, and the same number of drunks drive during each of the three periods.

The statistical test of the null hypothesis will actually use only the data shown in column 2 of Table 6.2, or the number of drunks observed during each time period. In our example 13 drunk drivers were observed during the 7-10 PM period. The χ^2 single sample test will statistically compare the actual number of drunks at each time period with the number of drunks that could be expected if time period (the independent variable) had nothing to do with the number of drinking drivers on the road. If this were the case, the same number of drunks should have been observed during each time period. This statistical comparison involves a number of computational steps (discussed in detail in the Appendix) that lead to a test statistic, the χ^2.

The statistical decision of whether to reject the null hypothesis is based on the value of the χ^2 statistic and the significance level (α) that the researcher has set for the investigation. Once again, the significance level is the probability of a Type I error and indicates the degree of confidence the experimenter feels he must have that the alternative hypothesis is correct. Let us assume that we have specified the .05 level as the significance level for our study and that we have calculated the χ^2 value for our data. The next step in the hypothesis-testing process is relatively simple and involves the use of a table of the χ^2 distribution, which can be found in most statistics texts. A simplified version of such a table is shown in Table 6.3. On the basis of our data, the χ^2 value is 24.24. To decide whether this figure is large enough to justify rejecting the null hypothesis, we must compare our χ^2 value with a critical χ^2 value found in the table under the column labeled .05 (significance level) and in row 2 (three time periods minus one equals two). If our χ^2 value is larger, we can reject the null hypothesis in favor of the alternative. If our χ^2 value is less than the critical value (5.991 in this case), we cannot reject the null hypothesis. Since our χ^2 of 24.24 exceeds the critical value of 5.991, however, we would reject the null hypothesis and conclude that the number of drunks

TABLE 6.3.   A portion of a table of the χ^2 distribution giving critical χ^2 values for various significance levels and numbers of cells compared.

Number of Cells Minus One	Significance Level		
	.10	.05	.01
1	2.705	3.841	6.635
2	4.605	5.991	9.210
3	6.251	7.815	11.345
4	7.779	9.488	13.277
5	9.236	11.070	15.086
6	10.645	12.592	16.812

who drive is influenced by the independent variable, time period. Note that our conclusion refers to the entire population of drunk drivers and is based on our estimation of the way this population is distributed by time of day from the sample we observed. We might, then, recommend to the police department that they schedule their patrol activity so as to be particularly observant for drunks during the later part of the 7 PM to 4 AM shift, since we demonstrated that they are likely to be in particularly abundant supply in the early morning hours.

The Sign Test

Behavioral researchers frequently encounter situations in which the design of their investigation is such that comparisons must be made between two groups of paired or matched subjects or between the performance of a single group of subjects tested on two different occasions. When this is the case and when the dependent variable is measured on the ordinal scale, the *sign test* is frequently chosen as the statistical technique for hypothesis testing.

Suppose, for example, that a researcher is interested in evaluating differences between the attitudes of husbands and wives toward the women's liberation movement. The sample for his study might consist of a number of husband-wife (or wife-husband, depending on one's attitude toward women's liberation) pairs. For a measure of the dependent variable, attitude toward the women's liberation movement, the researcher might ask each of the couples in the sample to respond separately to the following ordinal scale type of question:

Which of the following describes your opinion of the merit of the objectives of the women's liberation movement?
1. A ridiculous set of unreasonable demands by a bunch of frustrated old maids.
2. A largely irrelevant set of protests over relatively unimportant issues.
3. No opinion.
4. The expression of basically worthy concerns that touch on important aspects of modern life.
5. Clear statements of vitally necessary solutions to the most pressing problems affecting society.

The data obtained might look like those shown in Table 6.4. In this table each pair member (husband and wife) receives a score between 1 and 5 representing his or her attitude toward the question asked. In the last column of the table is the algebraic sign of the difference between the score of the husband and that of the wife in each pair. A minus sign indicates that the wife's attitude is more favorable toward women's lib, a plus sign indicates that the husband has the more positive attitude, and a zero indicates that both share the same attitude. These are the only data required for the statistical decision-making process that uses the sign test.

In our example six of the ten pairs of subjects show a minus sign, indicating that the husband's attitude is less positive than the wife's; two pairs show a plus sign; and two pairs show zero, or no difference in

TABLE 6.4.   Hypothetical data for a sign test: husbands' and wives' attitudes toward women's lib from a five-point rank order item. A 1 is the most negative and a 5 is the most positive attitude.

Pair Number	Attitude Scores Husband	Wife	Sign of Difference
1	1	3	−
2	1	5	−
3	4	5	−
4	3	3	0
5	5	3	+
6	2	4	−
7	3	5	−
8	3	2	+
9	4	4	0
10	2	3	−

attitude. The scientific hypothesis of this study might be of the following form:

> Wives exhibit a more positive attitude toward women's liberation than do their husbands.

This could be translated into the language of the sign test by the following alternative hypothesis:

> H_1:   A greater-than-chance number of minus signs result when husbands' and wives' attitudes toward women's lib are compared such that for each couple a minus is recorded if the wife's attitude is more favorable and a plus if the converse is true.

The null hypothesis would, of course, be the converse of the alternative hypothesis and might be of this form:

> H_0:   The probability of obtaining minus or plus signs from the comparison of the attitudes of husband-wife pairs is determined by chance, and we can expect (by chance) an equal number of pluses and minuses.

The statistical decision based on the sign test is again a simple and straightforward process. The investigator merely counts the number of minus signs in the comparisons and consults a statistical table containing critical values associated with the appropriate significance level and number of husband-wife pairs. If the number of minus signs exceeds the critical value, the investigator can safely reject the null hypothesis; if it does not, he cannot reject the null hypothesis and must dismiss the alternative hypothesis.

The Mann-Whitney U Test

The *Mann-Whitney* U *Test* for two independent samples is another of the more popular nonparametric, or distribution-free, tests and is one of the most powerful of all these techniques. By "powerful" we mean that this statistical test is capable of indicating rejection of the null hypothesis when it is false more frequently than other tests are able to do while maintaining equal significance levels and that it is sensitive to smaller differences than are other tests. The Mann-Whitney is appropriate for studies in which the research purpose is to demonstrate whether an independent variable will differentially affect two distinct and separate groups of subjects. Although two groups of subjects were used in our example of the sign test, these groups were not independent of each other, since a very specific type of relationship (marriage) associated the group of husbands with the group of wives. The Mann-Whitney U Test is suited to studies in which the two groups are selected independently.

As a nonparametric test the Mann-Whitney requires that the dependent variable be measured on at least the ordinal scale and, consequently, that it is possible to rank order the observations of the dependent variable. Although particularly suited for ordinal scale measures, the Mann-Whitney U Test is frequently used with interval scale data as a substitute for a parametric hypothesis test when the assumptions required for the parametric tests cannot be met.

To illustrate the Mann-Whitney U Test, let us assume that we have conducted a study with the following alternative hypothesis:

H_1: Patients receiving a therapeutic dose of tranquilizer X will exhibit a lower average anxiety rating than patients who receive no medication.

The converse of this prediction is stated by the null hypothesis:

H_0: No differences will exist between the average anxiety ratings of subjects who receive tranquilizer X and those who do not.

To provide a test of the null hypothesis with the Mann-Whitney U Test, we might design a study such that the treatment group and the control group are randomly selected from among the patients of a cooperating physician to eliminate any differences among the subjects of the two groups before the experiment took place. The treatment group would then be given tranquilizer X at the regular therapeutic dose; the control group would take no medication. After the treatment period both groups would complete the anxiety scale, and an ordinal scale score would be assigned to each subject depending on how he rates his anxiety level. We might observe the following outcome:

| Tranquilizer Group: | 10 | 30 | 20 | 50 | |
| Control Group: | 60 | 40 | 80 | 70 | 90 |

Each number represents the anxiety score of a particular subject in one of the two groups (four treatment and five control subjects).

As a first step in testing the null hypothesis, we might arrange all nine scores in a composite rank-ordered series and identify each score with its group:

10	20	30	40	50	60	70	80	90
T	T	T	C	T	C	C	C	C

We can see that the scores of the two groups of subjects range from a low of 10 to a high of 90 and that while most of the treatment group scores are at the low end of the series and the control group's at the high end, the lowest control group score is lower than the highest treatment group score. For very small samples such as this, computing the value of the U statistic is very simple. First, we count the number of times that a C score precedes a T score as we move from left to right in this distribution (from low to high scores). In our example only one T score is preceded by a C score—the C score of 40 precedes the T score of 50. This simple counting operation provides us with a value for the U statistic, in this case a U of 1. Next, we take the opposite tack and calculate a second U value by counting the number of T scores ded by three T scores, and the C scores of 60, 70, 80, and 90 are each preceded by all four T scores. Our second U value will therefore be given as:

$$U = 3 + 4 + 4 + 4 + 4 = 19$$

Although we calculate two separate values of the U statistic each time we conduct the Mann-Whitney, we always use the smaller of the two U values in the actual hypothesis test. The larger U is referrred to as U' and is not used in the test of the null hypothesis.

Having obtained our U value of 1, we again use a statistical table for the hypothesis test. This table contains critical U values for the particular significance level (α) and number of subjects tested in the treatment and control groups. In our example, with four treatment group and five control group subjects and a significance level of .05, we find by consulting the table that we can safely reject the null hypothesis if the obtained U is 2 or less. Since our U is 1, we can reject the null hypothesis and conclude that the tranquilizer does reduce the anxiety level of patients.

The computation of the U statistic and the application of the Mann-Whitney Test are simple procedures when the sizes of the two independent groups are small, as in our example. When large numbers of subjects are tested, however, slightly different computation procedures are used to simplify the task of the researcher. These steps are given in the Appendix, together with a more detailed account of the rationale for this nonparametric hypothesis-testing procedure.

PARAMETRIC HYPOTHESIS TESTS

Parametric tests of statistical hypotheses are generally the most powerful inferential techniques available to the behavioral scientist—that is, they are the most likely to lead to rejection of the null hypothesis when the alternative hypothesis is true. The reason for the superiority of parametric over nonparametric methods is very simple. The parametric tests of hypotheses make maximum use of the information contained in the data of a study. In virtually every case the parametric techniques use statistical indexes such as the mean, variance, and standard deviation. The results obtained with these techniques are difficult to interpret for nominal and ordinal scale data simply because the mathematical operations required for the computation of these statistics are not meaningful for nominal or ordinal measures.

Another characteristic distinguishing parametric from nonparametric hypothesis tests relates to additional assumptions made in the parametric tests. Perhaps the most important of these assumptions is that the dependent variable is normally distributed in the population of interest. By "normally distributed" we mean that the population mean is at the center of the distribution and that the distribution of dependent variable scores around this mean is symmetrical and characterized by the bell shape shown in Figure 6.1. In the normal distribution approximately 68 percent of the observations fall within one standard deviation unit of the mean, and the remaining 32 percent of the observations taper off toward the ends, or tails, of the distribution as shown in Figure 6.1.

To illustrate the general manner in which hypotheses are examined with parametric tests, we will briefly, and at a conceptual level, discuss two of the most frequently used parametric techniques, the t *test* and the *analysis of variance*.

The t *Test*

Independent Samples.   Two principal varieties of the parametric *t* test are available to the behavioral scientist. The first of these, the *t* test for independent samples, is the parametric equivalent of the Mann-Whitney *U* Test, described in the preceding section. As is that test, the *t* test is designed for those research situations in which distinct and separate groups of subjects are tested, as opposed to situations in which the same subjects are tested under separate conditions or in which matched groups of subjects are used. Although the general objective of the two hypothesis-testing procedures is the same, the *t* test approaches

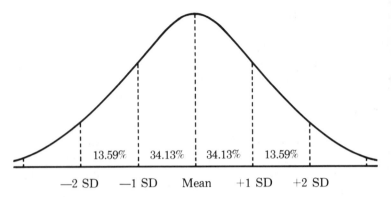

FIGURE 6.1. The normal distribution, showing the percentage of scores falling plus or minus one and two standard deviation units on either side of the mean.

the problem from a slightly different direction and uses the additional information contained in interval or ratio scale data to accomplish its purpose.

For an illustration of the t test for two independent samples, consider a study of the scientific hypothesis that children from higher socioeconomic class families are more intelligent than children from low socioeconomic class families. Because the purpose of our research is to make inferences about the effects of socioeconomic status (the independent variable) on intelligence (the dependent variable) in general rather than about the relatively small groups of subjects we might happen to test in our study, we might state the statistical and null hypotheses in the following form:

H_1: The mean intelligence of high socioeconomic class children, as measured by IQ test X, is greater than the mean IQ of low socioeconomic class children.

H_0: IQ is not affected by socioeconomic status, and the mean IQ scores of high and low socioeconomic status children are from the same population distribution.

To test the statistical hypothesis against the null hypothesis, we might proceed in much the same way that studies using nonparametric techniques are designed. We can randomly select two groups of subjects, one consisting of children from high socioeconomic status families and the other of children from low socioeconomic class families, and administer IQ test X to the children in each group. On the basis of these data, we compute the t statistic, which involves the calculation of the mean and standard deviation for each group. (The computational steps for this and other statistical tests can be found in the Appendix.) As with the other hypothesis tests we have discussed, the hypothesis-testing decision is based on the use of statistical tables containing critical t values for particular significance levels and group sizes. We compare the t value we have computed with a critical t value for a particular significance level (.05, for example) and reject the null hypothesis if our t is larger or accept the null hypothesis if our t is smaller.

As indicated by the wording of the alternative and null hypotheses, however, the t test represents a slightly different type of hypothesis-testing procedure than the Mann-Whitney U Test, for instance. Figure 6.2 represents conceptually the process involved in the t

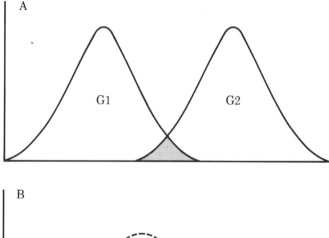

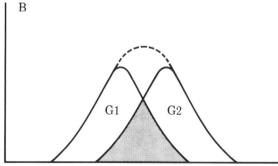

FIGURE 6.2.   A conceptual illustration of two possible t test outcomes. In part A the two groups (G1 and G2) show very little overlap (shaded area), and it is probable that the two are from different populations. In B, on the other hand, there is extensive overlap, and it is entirely possible that both G1 and G2 are samples from the distribution shown with the dashed line.

test we have described and illustrates two possible outcomes of our hypothetical study of IQ. The test is statistically concerned not only with assessing the difference between the means of the two socioeconomic groups, but also with the way that the IQ scores are spread out within each group, to determine whether the scores of the subjects within each group can best be considered as belonging to two different distributions (statistical hypothesis) or a single general IQ distribution (null hypothesis). The results depicted in section A of this figure would probably give rise to a statistically significant t test, or support rejection of the null hypothesis, primarily because there is very little overlap between the two distributions and because these data suggest that the IQ scores of the high and the low socioeconomic status children are from two different population distributions. The results shown in section B, on the other hand, would probably produce a t value that was not statistically significant, even though the mean IQs of the two groups are just as different as those shown in section A. This time, however, the two distributions show a great deal of overlap (shaded area), and it might be just as logical to conceive of the two groups we have tested as coming from the single distribution shown by the dotted line in this section. The t test is able to make this kind of distinction because, through the computation of the mean and standard deviation of the scores, it is using more of the information contained in the measures of the dependent variable than the nonparametric statistics use.

The t Test for Correlated Observations.   As we have indicated, the t test described previously is the parametric equivalent of the Mann-Whitney U Test, which is designed for research situations in which two distinct groups of subjects are tested. In contrast, the t test for correlated observations represents a parametric equivalent of the sign test and is designed for studies that compare the performance of the same subjects on different occasions or under different treatments or studies that use matched pairs of subjects. The following alternative and null hypotheses, for example, suggest the use of the correlated t test:

H_1:   The mean reaction time of individuals at a blood-alcohol concentration of .10 percent is greater than that under conditions of 0 percent BAC.

H_0:   The mean reaction times of humans is not different at BAC levels of .10 percent and 0 percent.

These hypotheses stipulate that a single group of subjects will be tested under two treatment conditions and that the two treatment conditions cannot be considered to be independent from each other, as was the case in the IQ example used in the previous section.

Although the computational steps for the *t* test for correlated observations differ from those required by the *t* test for independent groups, the final result, the *t* statistic, is treated in the same manner. Again, the obtained *t* value is compared with a critical value listed in a statistical table, and the decision to reject or not to reject the null hypothesis depends on whether the obtained *t* is larger than (reject the null hypothesis) or smaller than (accept the null hypothesis) this critical value for *t*.

Although the hypotheses used as an example for the correlated *t* test could be rephrased such that two independent groups could be tested (one with a .10 percent blood-alcohol concentration and the other with no alcohol), permitting the use of the *t* test for independent groups, the correlated *t* test design provides a better test of the hypotheses in this situation. The primary advantage of the matched pairs, or repeated measures design for which the *t* test for correlated observations is appropriate, is in the control of variation due to variables other than the treatment conditions under investigation. In the present example we have, by testing each subject under both an alcohol and a no alcohol condition, used each subject as his own control group. We would expect under these conditions that the performance of a given individual on two different occasions will be less variable, except for the influence of the independent variable (alcohol), than would the performance of two different individuals tested under different conditions. By selecting a repeated measures design, we have removed the possibility that individual differences among subjects will mask the effects of the independent variable. The repeated measures design is therefore more sensitive to the effects of the independent variable, since this is the only factor to which we can attribute differences in performance.

Analysis-of-Variance Techniques

Up to this point we have discussed statistical models for hypothesis testing that have, at most, compared the performances of two groups of subjects or of a single group tested on two occasions or under two different treatment conditions. Although these tests are useful for testing hypotheses concerned with such situations, behavioral scientists are frequently faced with research situations in which they wish to compare simultaneously more than two groups or more than two experimental treatments. In these more complicated research situations a variety of analysis-of-variance techniques are frequently used to test alternative hypotheses.

Like the t test, the analysis of variance is a parametric statistical test that uses the information contained in data measured on at least the interval scale of measurement. Also like the t test, the analysis-of-variance procedures require the computation of both means and measures of the variability of the interval or ratio scale data. Finally, as with the t test, this method attempts to determine statistically whether the measures recorded for different groups or under different treatment conditions are drawn from different distributions or merely represent different sets of observations drawn from a single distribution.

Assume, for example, that we wish to re-evaluate the question considered in our discussion of the t test for two independent samples. Instead of just comparing the IQ scores of low and high socioeconomic status children, we wish to include a third group of middle socioeconomic class children in the experimental design. Once again, we can graphically conceptualize this research situation as shown in Figure 6.3. Now instead of two distributions we have three, but the hypothesis-testing process is a fairly straightforward extension of the logic involved in the t test. The question asked with the application of the analysis of variance and its F test can be stated with the following hypotheses:

H_1: The mean IQ scores of high, medium, and low socioeconomic class children are not equal.

H_0: The mean IQ scores of high, medium, and low socioeconomic class children are equal.

Like the t test, the test statistic for the analysis of variance (the F ratio) is based on the means *and* variability measures derived from the three distributions of scores. Figure 6.3 shows three outcomes that could produce a statistically significant F ratio in the analysis of variance and a fourth outcome that probably would not lead to rejection of the null hypothesis. It should be noted, in connection with the three outcomes leading to rejection of the null hypothesis, that the analysis of variance does not indicate which group is different or that significant differences exist between each group, but rather that the three groups cannot be considered to be drawn from populations having the same means. In other words, if our study comparing the IQ scores of high, medium, and low socioeconomic class children produced a statistically significant F ratio, we would be led to reject the null hypothesis, which states that the means of the three populations are equal. We could not legitimately say, however, that a significant difference exists between any two of the population means. What we could do, however, in light of a finding of overall differences among the groups, is to conduct separate t tests for

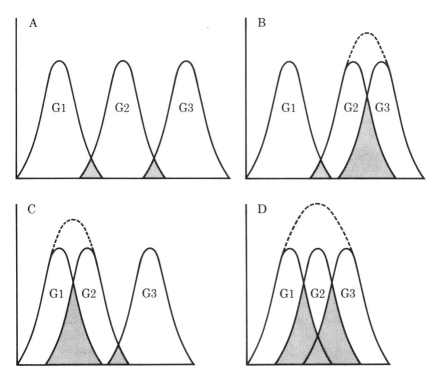

FIGURE 6.3.   A conceptual illustration of possible outcomes of an analysis of variance comparing G1, G2, and G3. Parts A, B, and C all show outcomes that could produce statistically significant differences, while part D shows a nonsignificant outcome. In A all three groups may be drawn from different populations, while in B and C only one of the three groups appears to be from a population different from the other two. In D, again, all three could very well be from the population described by the dashed line.

each pair of groups (high versus medium, high versus low, and medium versus low) in an attempt to determine where the differences did originate.[1]

The technique we have described (a simple one-way analysis of variance) is the simplest and most basic of a wide variety of analysis-of-variance models available to the behavioral researcher. More complex models allow tests of hypotheses in repeated measures designs, where the same subjects are tested under different experimental conditions. Still

[1]Alternative procedures are available, however, to provide for the isolation of the effects in the event of a statistically significant F ratio; see, for example, Winer (1971).

more complex models allow for the simultaneous tests of hypotheses involving several different independent variables in the same experiment. All these more complex forms of the analysis of variance share the basic features of the technique we have discussed, however. The more complicated forms of analysis are merely extensions of the basic parametric hypothesis-testing technique, which begins with the t test, to more complicated research problems. All these models are also structured to provide test statistics that can be compared to critical values found in various statistical tables, with the comparison resulting in a simple yes or no decision on rejection or nonrejection of the null hypothesis. In the event that the researcher is able to reject the null hypothesis, he has indirectly provided evidence for the acceptance of his alternative hypothesis.

THE INTERPRETATION OF RESEARCH RESULTS

Up to this point we have been primarily concerned with the objective and quantitative aspects of behavioral research. The statistical decisions we have made have been very clear-cut and automatic. If a test statistic equaled or exceeded a critical value obtained from the appropriate statistical table, the decision to reject H_0 in favor of H_1 was automatic. Conversely, if the test statistic failed to equal the critical value, the decision not to reject the null hypothesis was equally automatic. Now, however, we must consider the much more subjective process of interpreting research results, or figuring out what a study has told us. We will briefly discuss a few key issues in attaching scientific meaning to the results of behavioral research.

Practical versus Statistical Significance

One of the most important and yet most frequently ignored problems in the interpretation of the results of behavioral studies is the practical significance of the research findings. To both the researcher conducting behavioral studies and the reader studying the reports of research, it must be made very clear that *statistical significance in no way guarantees practical significance*. It is quite possible to design and conduct behavioral studies that statistically detect the most trivial differences between groups of individuals. Assume, for example, that we conducted a study comparing the reaction times of males and females and found that the difference in mean reaction time for the two groups is only .02 seconds, but that the result is significant at the α level of .01. It is entirely possible that a difference this small would be deemed significant, particularly if the groups were relatively large. It is extremely difficult, however, to imagine a situation in which a difference of .02 seconds would make any practical difference in the performance of either men or women. Every researcher owes it to himself and to those who will read or use his research results to give careful attention to interpreting his findings in terms of their practical meaning as well as in terms of their statistical significance.

Determining the practical significance of research findings can be approached on two different levels. On a statistical level, techniques do exist that assist the researcher in attributing practical significance to statistically reliable findings. It is possible with most of the parametric hypothesis-testing models, for instance, to compute statistical indexes that reflect the percentage of the variability among scores in a particular study attributable to the effects of the independent variable. These indexes are ordinarily calculated after the hypothesis test has been conducted and are primarily designed to assist and support the researcher in his interpretation of the research results.

On the other level, ascribing practical importance to statistically significant findings is still primarily a subjective, judgmental process. Although statistical tools may be useful in this process, the researcher has the ultimate responsibility for rendering a judgment on the practicality of his findings. It might also be noted that the consumer of reported research findings has a similar responsibility to be critical of the inferential process displayed by the researcher. That a journal article or technical report is replete with statistical tests showing significance at the .001 level is no guarantee that useful or meaningful information about behavioral processes has been produced. It should be kept in mind that in the scientific process statistical procedures are used as tools to gather evidence to support the judgment of the researcher. These statistical tools are as subject as any other tools to misuse. We might at this point profit from some old but still timely advice given by Guilford (1936):

> The sane attitude to take is to remember that statistical methods are merely helpful and significant tools and that the master craftsman remains the master of his tools; he never lets his tools become the master of him. If too often we find that figures fool, it is because too often fools figure [p. 12].

The Inferential Process

Another important consideration in the interpretation of research results is the inferential process involved in the various hypothesis tests we have considered. Recall that the ultimate statistical test employed has consistently been a test of the null hypothesis and that the statistical decision has uniformly been to reject or fail to reject it. On the basis of this statistical decision, the researcher then makes inferences about the alternative and scientific hypotheses, which gave rise to the null hypothesis. The decision about the alternative hypothesis is ordinarily reasonably straightforward, since the alternative and null hypotheses are, if properly stated, directly related; and if one is true, the other must be false. The real difficulty in the interpretation of research findings arises in the relationship between the statistical and the scientific hypotheses. Recall that the scientific hypothesis is ordinarily a relatively general statement of the relationship expected in a given study and that the statistical hypothesis is much more specific to the conditions of the study. It is important, in the interpretation and generalization of research results, that the statistical hypothesis is an accurate and comprehensive representation of the scientific hypothesis. Consider, for example, the following hypotheses:

Scientific hypothesis: Driving performance will be impaired by alcohol.

Alternative hypothesis: Drivers tested under a 0 percent blood-alcohol concentration will manifest a shorter mean response time to a simple reaction time test than will drivers tested under a .05 percent BAC condition.

The implication of a study conducted under these hypotheses is that acceptance or rejection of the alternative hypothesis will inferentially lead to acceptance or rejection of the scientific hypothesis. A serious question might be raised, however, about the relationship between the scientific and alternative hypotheses. Specifically, it is questionable that performance on a simple reaction time task can legitimately be generalized to the whole of driving performance.

Both the researcher and the consumer of research reports should be critical of overgeneralizations made on the basis of statistical tests applied to specific hypotheses.

Nonsignificance

It is not uncommon for the behavioral scientist to be faced with a situation in which the statistical evidence leads to the rejection of a favorite hypothesis. Unfortunately, the reaction to this turn of events is not as universally objective and impartial as one might expect from scientists. The frequently observed depression over failure to reject the null hypothesis is probably aggravated by the lack of interest the editors of scientific journals display toward the publication of studies yielding nonsignificant results. Failure to reject H_0 can, however, be scientifically meaningful; and this outcome requires scientific interpretation to the same degree that statistical significance does.

The first possibility the researcher should consider in interpreting nonsignificant findings is that they are real. If the study has been properly conducted, appropriate kinds of behavior measured, and the appropriate statistical analysis conducted, it is highly likely that failure to reject H_0 indicates that H_1 is untenable. Recall that the tenability of this result is reflected in the power, $1 - \beta$, of the statistical test. Nonsignificant research results can, however, have considerable scientific meaning. Suppose, for example, that we found that no statistically significant differences in efficiency could be detected between televised and direct contact teaching methods. This result may indicate that we can be about as confident in either method in terms of accomplishing educational objectives. On the basis of this failure to reject H_0, we might decide which method to use on the basis of other considerations, such as cost. If the televised teaching method was less expensive than direct contact methods, the nonsignificant result of our study could in fact save a particular school system considerable expense.

Although we should first consider the possibility that a nonsignificant result is a valid conclusion, it is also important to re-examine the design of the study before dismissing the alternative or scientific hypothesis as invalid. As we have seen in previous chapters, a number of factors can compromise the validity of a study and could lead to rejection of the alternative hypothesis when it is true. We must be concerned with the power of the statistical hypothesis test itself and its sensitivity to real differences. However, a number of factors can mask statistically significant differences even in the most powerful statistical hypothesis tests. Among these factors are the precision of the measurement applied to the dependent variable and the sample selection procedures. If the measure of performance is inappropriate or imprecise and the sample not representative, no statistical manipulation will save the study.

SUMMARY

Scientific hypotheses are relatively general statements about the types of effects or relationships expected in a particular study. They lead to the formulation of more explicit, statistical hypotheses, which are evaluated by hypothesis-testing procedures.

Statistical hypotheses are of two primary types, both of which involve parameters of the populations to which the scientific results are to be generalized. The alternative hypothesis is the positive statement of the effect or relationship expected, while the null hypothesis, or hypothesis of no effect, is the complement of the alternative hypothesis.

Hypothesis-testing procedures evaluate the null hypothesis and provide evidence that enables the researcher to reject or fail to reject the null hypothesis. Rejection of the null hypothesis implies support for its complement, the alternative hypothesis. Failure to reject the null hypothesis is not the same as accepting the null hypothesis.

Deciding whether to reject the null hypothesis confronts the researcher with two types of potential errors. A Type I error occurs when the investigator decides to reject the null hypothesis when it is true. The probability of this type of error is controlled by establishing a significance level (α) for the statistical test. A Type II error occurs when the statistical decision is to fail to reject the null hypothesis when it is actually false (the alternative is true). The probability of this type of error is symbolized by β, and the power of a statistical test, or its sensitivity to real effects, is $1 - \beta$.

Nonparametric, or distribution-free, statistical tests are particularly useful in situations in which measurement is on nominal or ordinal scales. These procedures may also be appropriate, however, for interval or ratio scale data. Nonparametric tests, such as the χ^2 single sample test, the sign test, and the Mann-Whitney U Test, evaluate differences in the distributions of sample observations and lead to inferences about the distributions of the populations from which the samples were drawn. Nonparametric tests are generally less powerful than comparable parametric tests.

Parametric statistical tests are primarily appropriate for measures taken on the interval or ratio scales and require more assumptions about the distribution of scores in the populations of interest than do the nonparametric tests. Parametric tests are, however, generally more powerful than nonparametric tests. Tests such as the t test for independent groups, the t test for correlated samples, and the analysis of variance are examples of frequently used parametric hypothesis tests.

Although statistical hypothesis tests are extremely important in providing sound quantitative evidence on the basis of which statistical—and, indirectly, scientific—hypotheses can be evaluated, the researcher is still obligated to interpret the findings of his research. The process of attaching practical significance to statistically significant findings is basically a judgmental enterprise and requires great scientific insight.

REPORTING
THE RESEARCH

7

Although the findings of a scientific investigation may add to the knowledge of the investigator, if they are not reported, they contribute very little to the field as a whole. Consequently, the last stage of the research process—reporting the findings—is critical.

The results of investigations are often unreported, at least not formally in the professional journals. Although no statistics on the ratio of reported to unreported studies exist as far as the authors are aware, it is probably safe to estimate that there are several unreported studies for every one that is reported in the journals. One of the reasons is that writing up the results of an investigation is not fun for most researchers. They probably enjoy the actual conducting of the study, but writing the report may be time consuming and often boring. Although those who have never written a scientific report may think that it is accomplished in a few hours, this is usually not the case. Sometimes a half-dozen or more drafts of the report are necessary before the writer is satisfied, so that weeks or even months of part-time writing are spent on the report. Thus, the findings of some studies are not reported simply because the investigator does not have the motivation to do the writing. However, when the research is funded by private or government agencies, progress reports and final reports are nearly always required, so the investigator is forced to write up his research. As we shall see later, reports of this type are often difficult for other investigators in the field to obtain and, in terms of impact on the scientific field, may not be much better than no report of the study at all.

When the data obtained in an investigation are analyzed, the differences between experimental conditions are frequently found to be statistically nonsignificant. Although in some types of studies this finding is meaningful and should be reported, in most instances researchers do not report findings of this type. Even if they attempted to do so, the editors of scientific journals are often reluctant to publish studies having statistically nonsignificant results. In some respects this attitude is unfortunate; much unnecessary research is conducted because investigators are unaware of other studies that answered the same research question but were not published because the findings were not significant.

Reports of other investigations are not published even though the findings are significant. Since the editors of most scientific journals receive many more manuscripts than they can publish, a sizable percentage of them are rejected. Although the editorial boards of the various journals would probably argue that all worthwhile investigations are published, investigators who have had manuscripts rejected might take a different view. Usually when a manuscript is rejected, if the author makes the changes recommended by the editors, it will be accepted for publication later. However, the initial rejection of a report in many instances results in the investigator's placing the manuscript in his file and not touching it again.

Regardless of the reasons an investigation does not get reported, when it does not it has contributed virtually nothing to the field. Consequently, the dedicated researcher makes every effort to present the findings of his investigation to the scientific community.

WHERE THE FINDINGS ARE REPORTED

Research findings are presented orally at professional meetings or are prepared for publication as a journal article, a technical report, a book, or some other form of publication. Although we cannot discuss all the various outlets available for reporting the results of research in the behavioral sciences, in this section we will briefly consider several of the more common.

Professional Meetings

Annually, hundreds of local, regional, national, and international professional meetings are held in which scientists present oral reports on their research. These meetings are sponsored by various societies and associations, and the reports presented at them certainly number in the thousands. Some of these meetings are quite small, while others, such as the annual American Psychological Association meetings, are attended by several thousand behavioral scientists. The list below of the major meetings held annually by psychological associations will give some idea of their number and diversity. This list includes only those meetings held in the United States; including international meetings would lengthen the list considerably. If the list were also expanded to include all the smaller meetings held by state psychological associations and by specialized groups of psychologists, it would indeed be formidable. Obviously, professional meetings serve as important outlets for publicizing research findings.

American Psychological Association
Southeastern Psychological Association
Western Psychological Association
Southwestern Psychological Association
Eastern Psychological Association
Rocky Mountain Psychological Association
Midwestern Psychological Association
Southern Society for Philosophy and Psychology
National Association of School Psychologists
American Society of Group Psychotherapy and Psychodrama
Annual Meeting of Mathematical Psychologists
Society for Clinical and Experimental Hypnosis

Although the above meetings are primarily for psychologists, many other disciplines are also interested in human and animal behavior and sponsor meetings in which research reports are given. For example, annual meetings of the American Sociological Association and the Rural Sociological Society are held primarily for their members to present research findings. At professional meetings held by anthropologists, political scientists, economists, and educators, to name only a few, papers dealing with behavior are also presented.

Typically, in preparing his report for presentation at a professional meeting, the researcher encounters a restriction that is not associated with many types of written reports. At nearly all meetings a person presenting a report is limited to ten or 15 minutes (sometimes less) to talk about his study. Often it is very difficult to present in a comprehensible form all the relevant information about a study in this time. All too often, the oral reports given at meetings are virtually incomprehensible, and the audience is left wondering what the investigator actually did and what his findings were. Fortunately, however, most groups that sponsor professional meetings also arrange to publish the proceedings of the meeting, so that the reports are also available in written form. Sometimes researchers giving oral reports at a meeting are required to submit more detailed written reports before the meeting convenes so that published proceedings will be available to the participants at the time of the meeting.

One major advantage of presenting a report at a professional meeting is that it permits an immediate interchange of ideas among the people working in a research area. Frequently the sessions at a meeting are set up in such a fashion that nearly as much time is allowed for audience discussion of a paper as is allowed for the presentation itself. Thus, an investigator often gets immediate feedback from his colleagues on their reactions to his research. In many instances these discussion periods become very heated, and although they can be traumatic for the investigator if he is unable to defend himself against some of the criticisms leveled, knowing that a study will have to be defended at a meeting probably serves to improve the quality of research.

Professional Journals

A large number of journals publish research findings in the behavioral sciences. The *Psychological Abstracts*, which abstract articles published in the journals that focus on the behavioral sciences, list over 450 publications from which the abstracts are obtained. Over 20,000 abstracts are published annually in this journal. Obviously, the amount of research conducted and reported in psychology and related sciences is substantial.

Before beginning to write up the findings of an investigation, the researcher typically decides to what journal he will submit the article for publication. Deciding on a particular journal before beginning writing is important, since various journals have different style requirements. Although a vast number of journals publish research in the behavioral sciences, the researcher typically has relatively few from which to choose. The reason is that journals have tended to become quite highly specialized, so that a given journal usually publishes articles dealing with a particular area of research. The area a journal is concerned with is often reflected in its name—for example, *Developmental Psychology, Journal of Abnormal Psychology, Journal of Comparative and Physiological Psychology, Journal of Personality and Social Psychology,* and *Journal of Educational Psychology*. Thus, an investigator usually selects a journal that he considers appropriate for the type of research project he has carried out.

Most journals have an editor and an editorial board made up of established investigators in the area of research in which the journal specializes. When the report of a study is submitted to the editor of the journal for publication, it is reviewed by several members of the editorial board for its scientific merit. Based on this review, a recommendation is made to accept or reject the article. Very often the acceptance of an article is contingent upon the author's making a number of changes that the board feels will substantially improve the quality of the manuscript. Sometimes the changes suggested are so extensive that the author must virtually rewrite the entire report.

There is currently some controversy over certain aspects of this review process. One of the main issues is the desirability of "blind" reviews. Typically, when an editor reviews an article and makes a recommendation to accept or reject it, he knows who wrote the article. Some researchers feel that this knowledge may bias the editors and that papers may sometimes be accepted because an editor is a friend of the author or because an author is so prominent that the editor hesitates to reject his paper. Consequently, several journals are now attempting the blind approach, in which the name of the author and the institution with which he is affiliated are removed from the article before it is given to the journal editors for review. Whether this practice will have any effect on the quality of the reports published by these journals remains to be seen.

One problem associated with publishing research reports in professional journals is the time lag between the date a report is initially submitted to a journal and the date when it is finally published. When the review time, the rewrite time, and the time involved in printing the article are all added together, the time lag may amount to as much as two years. Consequently, the new findings reported in journals are often not so new after all.

Technical Reports

A method of reporting research findings that has become increasingly common in recent years is the so-called technical report. Such reports are particularly common in the applied areas of research in which government agencies let contracts for specific projects. Also, many government and private laboratories publish their research findings in the form of technical reports. These reports may range from a few mimeographed pages to printed and bound reports of several hundred pages.

Publishing research findings in technical reports (or "tech" reports, as they are usually called) has advantages and disadvantages. An advantage is that there will not be the time lag associated with publishing in journals. Moreover, there is usually no space limitation in a technical report, so the investigator can describe his research and his findings in as much detail as he deems necessary. This is often not the case with articles published in a journal, for only a certain number of pages can be published in each issue. The primary disadvantage is that a technical report usually reaches a relatively small number of people. Although most organizations that publish research findings as technical reports have a mailing list of other researchers working in the same area, the distribution of these types of reports is quite limited.

Frequently the final report to a granting or contract agency is written in the form of a technical report. Although the investigator is usually free to distribute copies of these reports as he sees fit, sometimes distribution is restricted by the agency that supported the research. However, in most cases, not only is the investigator free to distribute the report but the granting agency, particularly if it is a federal government agency, makes copies of the report available for a nominal price through one of several government clearing houses. Thus, if an investigator wishes to obtain a copy of a technical report, he can usually do so. Possibly a bigger difficulty is in finding out about the study in the first place. At present technical reports are usually not abstracted, so that a researcher may not find out about research that has been conducted and reported by means of technical reports. However, a system is being developed that will result in the abstracts of many technical reports appearing in the *Psychological Abstracts*. This will result in a much wider dissemination of information appearing in technical reports.

In many instances an investigator who has reported a research project in a technical report also publishes an article on the same research in a professional journal. Most investigators feel that this practice does not violate the unwritten rule against double reporting of research. In double reporting a scientist publishes substantially the same report or the results from the same study in more than one journal. Doing so is considered unethical for several reasons. However, a technical report is usually not thought of as a published report, so if the same research appears in the form of a journal article, it is actually being published for the first time. This is also true of research reports given at professional meetings. It is common practice to present a report in oral form at a meeting and then later publish it in a journal.

Professional meetings, journals, and technical reports are probably the three major formal outlets for reporting research findings. However, a great deal of information about research is disseminated informally. For example many investigators attend professional meetings not only to listen to formal presentations of research findings but also to discuss with colleagues ongoing research and studies that have not been reported. Sometimes an investigator who, for various reasons, does not wish to report the findings of a study formally mimeographs or dittos a copy of the report and sends it to other investigators who may be interested. He frequently does this with a report that he hopes to publish eventually but that he thinks can be improved by feedback from colleagues. Although informal reporting of research findings should be the exception rather than the rule, it does serve a useful purpose.

WRITING THE REPORT

Writing a research report for publication requires a skill that most investigators learn only through considerable practice. Scientific articles usually require a blending of concision with clarity and conservation of space with adequate coverage that writers in the nonscientific fields do not have to achieve. Although some colleges and universities offer courses in scientific and technical writing and although books have been written on this subject, generally this skill is acquired only by doing and by having the product critiqued by colleagues or editors.

It is not the aim of this section to attempt to make a scientific writer out of the reader but rather to present in general terms some of the requirements of a good research report. Because various journals require different styles and formats, we cannot discuss the characteristics of a research report that would be acceptable in all journals. However, all the journals require much the same in the organization of a report and the type of information presented, and it is these aspects of report writing that we will discuss. Though perhaps not making a scientific writer out of the reader, this section should prove valuable for reading journal articles and other types of scientific reports.

We have already pointed out that the journal to which an investigator submits his research is to a great extent determined by the area in which the research was conducted. Usually the researcher is thoroughly familiar with the format of the journal and any unusual style requirements that it imposes. If not, before beginning his writing, he should familiarize himself with them. This can be done by looking at several articles in the journal and by reading the "Instructions to Authors" page included in most journals. Some organizations have published detailed guidelines for authors who plan to submit articles for publication by the organization. Thus, the *Publication Manual* (1967) of the American Psychological Association provides an author not only with detailed instructions on the preparation of his manuscript but also with information about the association's journals and publishing policy.

The journal that an article is being prepared for not only imposes formal style and organizational requirements but also influences the final version of the report in other ways. The potential reader of the article should be kept in mind at all times when writing the report, since an article that is highly suited to one type of reader may not be to another. In most cases an article is written with specialists working in the same narrow area in mind. Typically, readers of this type want detailed information about the results of the study and about the methods employed, so that they can duplicate the study if they wish. Sometimes, however, a report is written for a journal that is read by scientists in many different disciplines, so that a highly specialized article, such as might be submitted to a journal dealing with that particular specialized field, would not have much meaning for the readers. Thus, an article reported as the result of a particular piece of research would probably read quite differently if written for the *Journal of Experimental Psychology* than it would if it were written for *Science* or *American Scientist*, both of which are read by persons in a variety of disciplines. Although the best scientific writers can produce manuscripts that would appeal to a very wide audience, attempting to do this usually makes writing the research report, which is already a difficult job for many researchers, even harder.

The Organization of Research Reports

As we have indicated, the organization of research reports differs somewhat, depending on journal requirements. However, a report is usually broken up into sections and, perhaps, subsections, with each part containing a certain type of material. The body of the report generally consists of an introduction, a methods section, a results section, and a discussion section. In addition, a conclusion or summary section is often included, although many journals now require that an author submit an abstract of the article, which in most cases has taken over the function of the summary. Although these divisions are used for journal articles, most other types of scientific reports, including technical reports, follow this general format.

An article begins, of course, with a title and with the name of the author or authors and, usually, the institution where the research was conducted. These are often followed by the abstract of the article. This part of the report may appear to be straightforward and to present no problems, but sometimes this is not the case.

Title.   The title of an article provides a potential reader with his first cue to whether he will go on and read the article. Consequently, the title should give enough information about the contents of the article for the potential reader to make this decision. The title also should contain key words that can be used when the paper is eventually indexed in abstracts and other information systems. Since a title must be kept reasonably short, these requirements are often difficult to meet.

Authors. Often several individuals were involved in designing and conducting an experiment, and assigning credit to these people in an appropriate fashion may be a difficult task. As Wilson (1952) points out: "Here is a golden opportunity for losing friends. The decision as to what names should be included, and in what order, requires fair-mindedness and objectivity above the ordinary" (p. 358). Although the American Psychological Association's code of ethics contains some reasonably explicit rules for determining the order of names of authors on articles, and even who should be included as an author, the decisions are still somewhat arbitrary.

The investigator who contributed the most to the study or who had the primary responsibility for the investigation is generally listed first and is called the senior author. The person who contributed the next most is listed second, and so forth. If the investigators agree that all contributed equally, their names can be listed in alphabetical order. Sometimes individuals who helped with the study but did not make major contributions are not listed as authors but are acknowledged by means of a footnote. Obviously, deciding who did or did not make major contributions or who contributed the most could easily develop into a major misunderstanding. Usually, when several investigators are to be involved in a study, arriving at a decision on the order of authorship before the study is a wise procedure.

The reason the order of authorship is of particular importance is that usually the senior, or first, author of a paper receives the most credit for the work. In a system that places a great deal of weight on an investigator's publication list, being listed first is important. Being a junior author on a paper does not carry the same prestige as being the senior author.

On most papers after the authors' names is the name of the institution where the research was conducted. This name is listed even if the author is no longer at that institution. In this situation his present affiliation is usually indicated by means of a footnote. Since often a particular institution has a sizable investment in a piece of research, this system gives credit where credit is due.

Abstract. Most journals now require the author to submit an abstract of the article, which is usually printed above the body of the article. A well thought out abstract is important for several reasons.

Although the title of the report usually provides the first basis on which a potential reader decides whether to read the complete article, the abstract usually provides the final basis. The 200-words-or-less restriction that is frequently placed on the length of an abstract limits the amount of information that can be presented, but the abstract should give a reader an understanding of the objectives of the study, the types of subjects used, some idea of the methods employed, and the results. It is important that an abstract present the maximum amount of information possible in the space allowed because in many cases it is the author's abstract that is printed verbatim in an abstract journal. Although an author may assume that a reader has the article to refer to if the abstract is not clear, he does not when it appears in an abstract journal.

Introduction. As the name implies, the introduction of an article serves to introduce the reader to the research described. It generally acquaints the reader with the current status of research in the area, often presents a brief history of the previous work in the field, and includes references to the most relevant and up-to-date literature in the field. The introduction typically concludes with a statement of the question that the research was designed to answer.

Methods Section. This section, which usually includes several subsections, should describe the design of the study, the number and characteristics of the subjects, a description of the apparatus and special equipment, the techniques of measurement, and so forth. It may also contain a subsection describing the data analysis and the statistical techniques used in the analysis. Depending on the type of the study, the methods section may be the longest part of the report. However, regardless of the length, the criterion for a good methods section is that it presents enough detail so that another researcher who reads the article can duplicate the study if he wishes.

Results Section. In this section the data from the study and the results of the analysis of these data are given. The data are usually presented in a summarized form by means of tables, graphs, and charts, and some thought must be given to making these as comprehensible as possible to the reader. If the statistical techniques used were not described in the methods section, a description of these should be included and the results of these analyses, often given in the form of a table, presented.

Frequently an author is tempted to begin to discuss or interpret the results in this section. Doing so is generally inappropriate. Sometimes, however, in short articles the results section is combined with the discussion section.

Discussion Section.   The purpose of this section of the report is to interpret the results of the study. Typically, the author discusses what he considers to be the limitations of the study and compares and contrasts his findings with those of other investigators or with widely held points of view in the field. The possible implications of the findings for theory or application are also discussed.

In some journals the discussion section is followed by a summary, although articles in journals that require an abstract usually do not have a summary. The last section of a report is typically the reference section, which includes all the material referred to in the article. The exact format for references differs among the journals not only in how they are listed in the reference section but also in how they are cited in the text of the article. This is another style point that an author should check on before beginning to write a report.

A Comment on Report Writing

We have stressed that the primary function of a scientific report is to communicate information about research. Frequently, in reading journal articles, one feels that the writer was making a conscious effort to confuse the reader and obscure the methods and findings of the study. Wilson (1952) remarks:

> Does the writer really want to convey information to his readers, or is he trying to impress them with his own genius? Unfortunately, some scientists suffer from an inferiority complex which continually compels them to bolster their egos by writing papers so obscure that even the most brilliant specialists in the same field cannot understand them. What a triumph! Naturally some subjects are much harder to make clear in a limited space than others, but very often obscurity is subconsciously deliberate. If a bit of reasoning was originally difficult for the author, it will almost certainly be difficult for many of his readers. The fact that long familiarity has rendered it obvious at last to the author is no excuse for his forgetting his earlier struggles or attempting to hide them [pp. 357–358].

Actually, it is more difficult to write an article that is "simple" and easy to understand than one that is characterized by excess technical terms and general verbiage. Although an article that is written in such a way as to make the obvious seem profound may impress a few readers, particularly those who have not had experience in writing, it will not impress the more sophisticated researchers among the readers.

The Last Steps in the Publishing Process

After an article has been written, it is submitted to the appropriate journal. We have already mentioned that journals have editorial boards that carefully review the article and decide whether it should be flatly rejected, accepted subject to various changes, or accepted as is. After the final version of the manuscript has been accepted, the editor turns it over to the company that does the actual printing of the journal.

After a considerable delay, often many months, the author receives a printed version of his manuscript called galley proofs and usually the original manuscript against which to compare the proofs. Often the proofs contain typesetting errors, omissions, and other kinds of mistakes, so it is important that the author do a very careful job of proofreading. After making corrections, he returns the proofs and the manuscript. Usually the author is allowed only a short time to read, correct, and return the proofs, since at this stage the printers are generally working on a tight time schedule.

Sometimes a second set of proofs is sent to the author. These are called page proofs and reflect the changes and corrections made in the galley proofs. Generally, page proofs are nearly error free. After he returns these proofs, the author sits back and waits for his article to appear in the journal.

A journal contains articles by a number of different authors. Typically, a number of copies of each of the articles are also printed separately and supplied to each author free or at a reasonable cost. These are called reprints and form the basis for an important exchange of information among scientists. Since there are virtually thousands of journals, no investigator can afford to subscribe personally to even a fraction of those he might wish to use to keep abreast of his field. Consequently, an article published in a journal that he does not subscribe to may be called to his attention by an abstract, references in other reports, or a variety of other ways. The investigator then writes to the author of the article of interest and requests a reprint. Most investigators in a few years build up extensive files of reprints, which, when indexed and cross-referenced, provide them with an extremely valuable source of information.

In this chapter we have stressed the importance of the reporting stage of the research process. We have emphasized that making the findings of a study available to the scientific community is essential if the research is to have any real value. It was also mentioned that reporting the results of his research is important to an investigator in that his advancement—promotions, raises, and so on—may depend to a large degree on his publications. What we have not mentioned, however, is the intrinsic satisfaction associated with ·the reporting process. Seeing the results of perhaps several years of research effort in the form of an article in a professional journal makes all the effort seem worthwhile. For most investigators, even those with numerous publications, opening a newly received journal and finding their long-awaited article is a rewarding experience.

THE STUDY OF BEHAVIOR—AN OVERVIEW

In the preceding chapters we have seen that the study of the wide range of activities we label behavior is not a simple task and requires the use of sophisticated methods. Although research methodology is a complex topic, the aim of this textbook has been to give the reader a basic understanding of the methods used by researchers in their study of behavior. For the reader who plans no further study of research methods and experimental design, this understanding should prove useful in reading about research in any of the disciplines concerned with human behavior. For those who will be taking advanced courses on research methods, this understanding should provide a solid foundation for their advanced work.

In this text we have viewed research on human behavior as consisting of a number of stages. Although it has been pointed out that the significance of each of these stages differs according to the particular research question to which an answer is being sought, typically all are involved in any investigation. In concluding our discussion of methods in the study of behavior, by way of an overall summary, let us again consider these various phases of the research process and some of the decisions that an investigator must make in designing and conducting his experiment.

An initial step in any investigation is the formulation and statement of the research problem. Just having an idea for a research project is not sufficient, since the idea may be only a general and confused notion. Transformation of this initial idea into a precise statement of a research problem, or question, that is amenable to scientific research is critical if the research is to be successful. Usually, the formulation and statement of the research problem are preceded or followed by an extensive review of the scientific literature in the area of interest. This review is another important phase of the research process.

After the investigator has transformed his initial idea into a workable statement of research, he designs an investigation that will answer the research question. In many instances the research question is such that deciding what research method to use is simple. However, in other cases the researcher may have to decide whether the experimental method, the testing method, or the systematic observation method will be most appropriate. If the experimental method is selected, he must decide on the most relevant dependent variable (or variables) to employ and must consider the question of its quantification to permit the statistical analysis of his research results. Although the independent variables in the investigation will be largely determined by the research question, the researcher must decide how these variables will be presented and manipulated in order to study their effects on the dependent variable. He must also decide on the type and number of subjects to be used and on how to select and assign them to the various conditions of his experiment. If the testing or systematic observation method has been selected for the investigation, the researcher will have other decisions to make. The end result may be a relatively simple and straightforward experimental design involving few variables or a more complex design calling for the simultaneous evaluation of the effects of a number of variables.

The investigator must keep another important consideration in mind in designing his study. There is a growing concern about the misuse of subjects—both human and nonhuman—in psychological research. If the investigator plans to use human subjects, he must be certain that his study will not expose his subjects to any physical or psychological damage. Precautions must also be taken when nonhuman subjects are employed to ensure that they are not exposed to needless pain or discomfort.

Once the researcher has made the decisions listed above and has designed his study, in some instances he is ready to conduct the investigation. However, very frequently there is another important stage between designing the study and carrying it out. This is the funding stage. Research is frequently expensive, so the investigator must attempt to obtain the necessary funds to carry out his study. He can try to obtain the funds in a number of ways, but the most common procedure is to prepare a research proposal which presents the research question and the design of the study in some detail, and submit this proposal to an agency that supports research. If the study is funded, the investigator is then ready to begin.

Once the study has been carried out, the data obtained are subjected to statistical analysis. This is the next stage of the research process. The particular statistical analysis employed will depend on the design of the study and the measures of the dependent variable obtained. Basically, however, through the appropriate application of statistical tests, the researcher can evaluate the truth or falsity of specific statements, or hypotheses, about behavioral processes.

The last phase of the research process is an important one. If the findings of an investigation are not reported, they contribute very little to the field as a whole. Consequently, after the study is completed and the data analyzed, the researcher must disseminate the information obtained from the study. Often this is accomplished by writing up the study for publication in a scientific journal or by presenting the findings at a professional meeting. However, the findings may also be reported in technical reports or in final reports to granting agencies. But regardless of how the findings are reported, it is important that they be made available to the scientific community.

APPENDIX:
DESCRIPTIVE
AND INFERENTIAL
STATISTICS

The material presented in this Appendix is intended to supplement the nonquantitative discussion of statistical methods found in the preceding sections of the book. The coverage of statistical methods presented here is not intended to be exhaustive or to serve as a manual for the conducting of detailed statistical analyses of research data. Instead, the Appendix illustrates some of the statistical procedures encountered in our survey of the research process. Although we will use and manipulate numbers to illustrate various statistical procedures, the only prerequisite to this material is a basic grasp of routine arithmetic operations (adding, subtracting, multiplying, and dividing) and an elementary knowledge of algebra.

The Appendix is presented in two principal sections, corresponding to a logical division of statistical methods into two primary functions: mathematically describing sets of research data and making inferences about populations or behavioral phenomena from research results.

DESCRIPTIVE STATISTICS

As we have indicated in various sections of this book, the research process involves, as a central element, the quantification of various types of behavior (dependent variables) according to specific sets of measurement rules. The type of measurement obtained will, of course, depend on the particular set of rules governing the manner in which numbers are assigned to our observations. In Chapter 2 we discussed four scales of measurement (or sets of quantification rules): the nominal, ordinal, interval, and ratio scales. In the present section we will be concerned with ways in which measures of these types can be statistically evaluated to describe or summarize the results of behavioral studies.

Measures of Central Tendency

The simplest type of descriptive statistic available to the researcher for summarizing a set of data is an average, or a single number that provides the best reflection of an entire group of observations of the dependent variable selected for study. There are, however, a number of different types of statistical averages, and the appropriate one to use in a particular situation is primarily determined by the scale of measurement used.

The Mode. The simplest statistical average we can use to summarize a group of observations is the mode. The mode is simply the most frequently occurring measurement category, and the only mathematical operation required to compute the mode of a distribution of scores is simple counting. Although the mode can be used as an average for data representing any of the four scales of measurement, it is the only permissible measure of the central tendency of nominal scale data.

The Median. Another index of central tendency is available to summarize data having at least ordinal scale properties. This measure is the median, or the midpoint of a set of scores. This type of statistical average is the score above which and below which 50 percent of the observations in a particular distribution will fall. The calculation of the median for a distribution of scores is only slightly more complicated than is the computation of the mode. The first step in calculating the median from a set of individual scores (which must, of course, represent at least ordinal measurement) is to arrange the scores in numeric order from smallest to largest. If the distribution contains an odd number of scores, the median is found by adding one to the number of subjects and dividing by two. Thus, if there are 15 subjects in our distribution, we would obtain:

$$\frac{15 + 1}{2} = 8$$

The median in this case would be the score obtained by subject 8 in our ordered distribution of scores. If the number of subjects is even, the median is defined as the point midway between the scores of the two subjects at the center of the distribution, or between subject $N/2$ and subject $(N/2) + 1$. Thus, if $N = 10$, the median is obtained by adding the scores of individual 5 $(N/2)$ and individual 6 $[(N/2) + 1]$ and dividing the sum by two.

The Mean.   The mean is the simple arithmetic average of a set of observations and is obtained by adding the set of observations and dividing by the number of observations made. This summary statistic is very useful with interval or ratio scale measurement but is not meaningful when applied to data collected through the application of a less rigorous scale of measurement. It would be ridiculous, for example, to compute the mean religious preference of a group of subjects, since this dependent variable can be measured only on the nominal scale. Even if we assigned a number to each of the various religions that served as category labels, it would make very little sense to say that the average religious preference of a group of individuals falls between the Protestant and Catholic categories.

The mean is a very important measure, however, when our measurement satisfies the rules of the interval or the ratio scale. It may make a great deal of sense, for instance, to speak of mean reaction time or mean running speed, since these measures can be assumed to have at least interval scale properties. The mean is usually symbolized as $\bar{X}$, and the computational formula is

$$\bar{X} = \frac{\Sigma X}{N}$$

where X represents the score obtained by an individual and Σ refers to the operation of summing all the X values. N denotes the number of individuals or observations. For example, if we have five scores (5, 6, 8, 10, and 11), the mean is computed as $(5 + 6 + 8 + 10 + 11)/5$ and equals 8.

Measures of Variability

The various measures of central tendency that we have discussed provide the behavioral scientist with a set of convenient tools to summarize one aspect of a given distribution of measures. These indexes—the mean, median, and mode—indicate the most likely value of the measured behavior or the average category of response. Frequently, however, the experimenter wishes to assess different characteristics of his data. One such characteristic is the way in which scores are distributed among individuals, or the extent to which the scores of different individuals tend to vary.

The Range. The simplest and most straightforward measure of this characteristic of a set of data is the range, or the difference between the highest and lowest scores observed. The range is an index of the maximum variability within a set of scores, or the amount of difference between the two extreme scores from the distribution. The range for the hypothetical data in Table A.1 is 3.

Deviation Scores. Although the range may be a suitable measure of variability, or the spread of scores, for some purposes (for example, ordinal scale data), if we are dealing with data having at least interval

TABLE A.1.   A set of hypothetical data illustrating the computation of various measures of variability.

Subject	Score	d	d^2
1	5	-1.5	2.25
2	5	-1.5	2.25
3	6	$-.5$	.25
4	6	$-.5$	.25
5	6	$-.5$	.25
6	7	$.5$	.25
7	7	$.5$	.25
8	7	$.5$	.25
9	8	1.5	2.25
10	8	1.5	2.25

$N = 10$ $\Sigma X = 65$ $\Sigma d = 0$ $\Sigma d^2 = 10.50$

$\overline{X} = 6.5$ $s^2 = (10.50)/10 = 1.05$

$s = \sqrt{1.05} = 1.025$ range $= 8 - 5 = 3$

scale properties, it may be more helpful to assess each score's deviation from the mean of the distribution. The mean of the hypothetical scores listed in Table A.1 is 6.5. The third column of this table contains the deviation score for each subject, or the difference between his score and 6.5. These deviation scores show us the distance of each raw score from the mean, but we are still left with as many separate numbers as we started with and do not have a single index that represents the spread, or variability, of the scores.

At first it might seem like a good idea to compute a mean deviation score by summing the second column of Table A.1 and then dividing by ten, the number of observations. We find when we try this approach, however, that the sum of the deviation scores will always be zero and the mean deviation will always reduce to O/N. The reason is that the mean is the arithmetic center of the distribution of scores, and the sum of the scores above the mean will always equal the sum of the scores below the mean. Thus, in our example the $+4.5$ (sum of the scores larger than the mean) is canceled out by the -4.5 (sum of the scores less than the mean), producing a zero sum.

The Variance and Standard Deviation. To circumvent the difficulty of the deviation scores summing to zero, we square each deviation score and then compute a mean square deviation, or variance, for the distribution of scores. The variance, or mean square deviation, is just what the name implies—the mean of the squared deviations of each score from the mean of the distribution. Column 4 of Table A.1 contains the squares of the deviation scores shown in column 3. The variance for this distribution is the sum of column 4 divided by the number of subjects, or 1.05. Thus,

$$s^2 = \frac{\Sigma d^2}{N}$$

An alternative method for computing the variance is given by the following formula:

$$s^2 = \frac{\Sigma X}{N} - \overline{X}^2$$

where $\Sigma X^2 =$ the sum of each score squared

$\quad\;\; N =$ the number of subjects

$\quad\;\; \overline{X}^2 =$ the square of the mean of the distribution

The standard deviation is simply the square root of the variance. For example, $s = \sqrt{1.05} = 1.025$.

Correlation

Occasionally in behavioral research more than one dependent variable is of interest to the investigator, and the research question involves the determination of the degree to which two or more measures of behavior are related or tend to measure the same attribute. The statistical index of the relationship between variables is the correlation coefficient, which provides, with a single numerical index, an important measure of the relationship between two dependent variables.

Fundamental to the determination of the relationship between two variables is the statistical concept of *covariance*. Very simply, covariance is the extent to which the two variables tend to vary together in value across subjects. If, for example, we administer two IQ tests to a group of subjects, we might obtain data like those shown in Table A.2. In this case the scores of the tests vary in exactly the same way across individuals. Those persons scoring high on test 1 also score high on test 2 and vice versa. In a case such as this, we observe a perfect relationship, or correlation, between the tests. Since this is a direct relationship (high scores on one test associated with high scores on the other, and low scores associated with low scores), we have a positive correlation. It is also possible to observe exact covariance between two sets of scores when the relationship is inverse. This is illustrated in Table A.3. In this situation we again have a perfect correlation between the tests, but the correlation is negative because the relationship is inverse; high scores on the first test are associated with low scores on the second and vice versa.

TABLE A.2.   An example of perfect positive correlation between two hypothetical IQ tests administered to ten subjects.

	IQ Scores	
Subject	*Test 1*	*Test 2*
1	130	128
2	128	126
3	117	115
4	115	113
5	109	107
6	109	107
7	106	104
8	103	101
9	102	100
10	100	98

TABLE A.3. An example of perfect negative correlation between two dependent variables. Notice the inverse relationship between the test scores.

Subject	Test 1	Test 2
1	90	40
2	80	50
3	70	60
4	60	70
5	50	80

The correlation coefficient, the statistical index of correlation, is usually designated as r. The value of r may range from $+1.00$, which indicates a perfect positive correlation, through zero, which indicates the absence of a linear relation between the two variables, to -1.00, which indicates a perfect negative correlation. The way in which the correlation coefficient is computed depends again on the scale of measurement that has been applied to the measured behavior. Different techniques are employed for ordinal than for interval or ratio scale data, and different computations are necessary when the measurement of one variable is ordinal and the other dependent variable has interval or ratio scale properties. We will briefly discuss the computational steps for each of these cases.

Ordinal Scale Correlation. If both of the variables whose relationship is assessed represent measurement on the ordinal scale, we can determine the relationship between these measures by computing the Spearman Rank Correlation Coefficient. Computation of this measure of correlation requires that both variables be measured on at least the ordinal scale of measurement, so that the scores for each variable can be ranked from greatest to smallest.

Suppose, for example, that we are interested in determining the relationship, or correlation, between the ratings of two job supervisors for ten individuals who work under them. We might ask each supervisor to *rank order* the employees according to his opinion of their effectiveness. The employee judged to be most proficient would receive the rank of 1 and the least proficient the rank of 10. When this rating was completed, we would have two ordinal scales similar to those shown in columns 2 and 3 of Table A.4, one scale for each supervisor.

Our task now is to determine the degree to which the two supervisors' ratings of the employees agree, or are correlated. To calculate r_s, the Spearman Rank Correlation Coefficient, from these data,

TABLE A.4.   A comparison of the ratings of ten employees by two supervisors. Each set of ratings consists of a rank ordering of the individuals from most to least proficient. The column headed d indicates the size of the difference between the rankings of the supervisors. The d^2 column contains the squared difference scores. These data produce an r_s of .939.

		Rankings		
Employee	Supervisor 1	Supervisor 2	d	d^2
1	9	8	1	1
2	5	5	0	0
3	1	2	1	1
4	2	1	1	1
5	3	4	1	1
6	6	6	0	0
7	10	9	1	1
8	4	3	1	1
9	7	7	0	0
10	8	10	2	4

$N = 10$ $\Sigma d = 8$ $\Sigma d^2 = 10$

we must first obtain a difference score (d) for each subject. The d is the difference between the rankings given a subject by the two supervisors. These are shown in the fourth column of Table A.4. The last column of Table A.4 contains the squares of these difference scores, which are used in the actual computation of the correlation coefficient. The formula for the computation of the Spearman r is

$$r_s = 1 - \frac{6\Sigma(d^2)}{N^3 - N}$$

where Σ = summing the values of d^2 (see bottom of column 5 in Table A.4)
  d^2 = the squared difference between the two supervisor rankings
  N = the number of employees (ten)
  N^3 = 10^3, or 1000

This formula gives the following for our example:

$$r_s = 1 - \frac{6(10)}{1000 - 10}$$

$$= 1 - \frac{60}{990}$$

$$= 1 - .061$$

$$= .939$$

Thus, the agreement, or correlation, between the rankings of our two supervisors is very high, and we would be inclined to conclude that the ranking technique was highly *reliable* with respect to these two individuals. As we have seen, the Spearman formula uses d, or the difference score between the two rankings for each individual, as a key to the computation of the correlation coefficient. It should be apparent that in the case of a perfect positive correlation ($r_s = 1$) both sets of ranks would be identical, and each of the ten difference scores would be zero, giving:

$$r_s = 1 - \frac{6(0)}{1000 - 90}$$

$$= 1 - \frac{0}{990}$$

$$= 1 - 0 = 1$$

On the other hand, if the two supervisors had been exactly opposite in their rankings, we might have obtained the result shown in Table A.5, which produces a perfect negative correlation. When the two sets of rankings are exactly the opposite of each other, the d's assume

TABLE A.5. An example of an exact inverse relationship between the rankings given by two supervisors, producing a perfect negative correlation ($r_s = -1.00$).

	Ranks			
Employee	*Supervisor 1*	*Supervisor 2*	*d*	*d²*
1	1	10	9	81
2	2	9	7	49
3	3	8	5	25
4	4	7	3	9
5	5	6	1	1
6	6	5	1	1
7	7	4	3	9
8	8	3	5	25
9	9	2	7	49
10	10	1	9	81

$N = 10$ $\Sigma d = 50$ $\Sigma d^2 = 330$

their largest possible values, as do the squared difference scores. These figures yield the following in the computation of the correlation:

$$r_s = 1 - \frac{6(330)}{1000 - 10}$$

$$= 1 - \frac{1980}{990}$$

$$= 1 - 2$$

$$= -1$$

It should be noted at this point that the raw data, representing the measurement of the two variables to be correlated, need not be in the form of a rank-ordered series to allow the computation of r_s. What is necessary is that the basic measures be taken on at least an ordinal scale and that it be possible to rank order the individuals on the basis of their scores to form a rank-ordered series. Suppose, for example, that we administer two short questionnaires to a group of individuals and that we wish to compute the correlation between the two. Each questionnaire contains five items, and there are five possible responses to each item. We can calculate a score for each individual on each questionnaire by simply assigning a number from 1 to 5 to the responses for each item and adding the numbers for the five items on each questionnaire together. By doing so, we might obtain data similar to those in columns 2 and 4 of Table A.6. From these data we can obtain the ranks shown in columns 3 and 5 of the table by arranging the scores from the two questionnaires in order of size. We can then calculate difference scores from columns 3 and 5 and proceed to compute r_s with the same formula we used earlier. Tied scores, such as that between individuals 4 and 5 on questionnaire 2, are handled by adding the two (or more) ranks involved (ranks 4 and 5), dividing by the number of individuals tied for that rank, and assigning the result to each individual. In this case both subjects are assigned the rank of 4.5. If relatively few ties occur, the formula given earlier for r_s can be used in the computation of the correlation coefficient. If a large number of tied scores occur, the correlation coefficient (r_s) calculated by this formula will tend to overestimate the real correlation between the variables, and a more involved formula to correct for ties should be used (see Siegel, 1956). Ordinarily, however, the effect of ties on r_s is not great, and we will generally use the formula given.

TABLE A.6.   Calculation of ranks from raw data that are not rank ordered. The d is the difference between columns 3 and 5 for each individual.

| | Questionnaire 1 | | Questionnaire 2 | | | |
Individual	Raw Score	Rank	Raw Score	Rank	d	d^2
1	25	1	20	2	1	1
2	20	2	15	3	1	1
3	15	3	25	1	2	4
4	10	4	10	4.5	.5	.25
5	5	5	10	4.5	.5	.25

$N = 5$ $\qquad\qquad\qquad\qquad\qquad\qquad\qquad\qquad$ $\Sigma d = 5$ $\quad$ $\Sigma d^2 = 6.5$

$$r_s = 1 - \frac{6(6.5)}{125 - 5} = 1 - .325 = .675$$

Interval and Ratio Scale Correlation.   We have described a procedure for assessing the degree of relationship between two ordinal scale variables. The Spearman technique provides an excellent means of assessing correlation when our measures are taken on an ordinal scale, but the technique is inappropriate if our measures of the dependent variables satisfy the conditions of the interval or ratio scales of measurement. Although it is possible to compute r_s for two interval scale measures by following the procedures illustrated in Table A.6, the correlation formulas designed for interval scale data are more appropriate when we have interval or ratio scale data.

The most frequently used interval or ratio scale correlation method is the Pearson Product Moment Correlation Coefficient, r. In calculating the Pearson Product Moment Correlation Coefficient, we will be dealing primarily with three different measures of the variability of the scores of one group of individuals on two measures of behavior. Our purpose, of course, is to determine the relationship between the two behavioral measures. Pearson's r is in fact a relatively simple ratio of these variability measures:

$$r = \frac{\text{covariance of } X \text{ and } Y}{(\text{standard deviation of } X)(\text{standard deviation of } Y)}$$

where X and Y are the two measures of behavior whose relationship we wish to assess and each individual receives one X and one Y score. The standard deviation of X is given as s_x, which, from our earlier discussion of measures of variability, is equal to

$$\sqrt{s_x^2}$$

or the square root of the variance of the distribution of X scores across individuals. Similarly, the standard deviation of Y equals

$$\sqrt{s_y^2}$$

Thus,

$$r = \frac{\text{covariance of } X \text{ and } Y}{\left(\sqrt{(\Sigma X^2/N)} - \overline{X}^2\right)\left(\sqrt{(\Sigma Y^2/N)} - \overline{Y}^2\right)}$$

where N = the number of individuals obtaining scores on variables X and Y

ΣX^2 = the sum of the squares of the X scores across all N individuals

ΣY^2 = the sum of the squares of the Y scores across the same N individuals

$\overline{X}$ = the arithmetic mean of the distribution of X scores (the sum of the X scores divided by N)

$\overline{Y}$ = the arithmetic mean of the distribution of Y scores

Thus,

$$r = \frac{\text{covariance of } X \text{ and } Y}{s_x s_y}$$

where s_x and s_y are the standard deviations of the X and Y score distributions respectively.

We see, then, that the denominator of the correlation formula is simply the product of the standard deviations of the two distributions of scores. These are measures of the extent to which the X's and the Y's vary, or are spread out independently of one another. The numerator of the formula is a third measure of variability, which is an index of the covariance of the X's and Y's, or the extent to which X and Y scores tend to vary together in value across individuals. That is:

$$\text{covariance of } X \text{ and } Y = \frac{\Sigma XY}{N} - \overline{X}\overline{Y}$$

Here ΣXY represents the cross-products of the X's and the Y's and is obtained by multiplying each individual's X and Y score together and summing the products across all N individuals. The expression $\overline{X}\overline{Y}$ in this equation is obtained by multiplying the mean of the X distribution of scores by the mean of the Y distribution. We can see from the above that the covariance of X and Y is obtained in a manner exactly analogous to the calculation of the variance of the X distribution or the Y distribution separately. Instead of the sum of the X's or Y's squared, we now use the cross-products of the X's and Y's, and instead of $\bar{X}^2$ or $\bar{Y}^2$, we use the product of $\bar{X}$ and $\bar{Y}$ to compute the covariance. Finally, then, we have as a formula for the Pearson Product Moment Correlation:

$$r = \frac{\Sigma XY/(N - \bar{X}\bar{Y})}{s_x s_y}$$

Let us illustrate these computational steps with a simple example. Suppose that we have developed a new IQ test and wish to determine the extent to which it is correlated with, or tends to measure the same thing as, an established IQ test. We might select a group of subjects and administer both tests to each subject. Assuming that both tests measure intelligence on at least an interval scale, we might obtain data similar to those shown in Table A.7. We then proceed to compute the Pearson r for these data. We can first compute the denominator of the expression as follows:

TABLE A.7.   Table for the calculation of the correlation between two hypothetical IQ tests administered to ten subjects.

| Subject | New Test Score | | Established Score | | Cross-Products |
	X	X²	Y	Y²	XY
1	95	9025	100	10,000	9500
2	120	14,400	115	13,225	13,800
3	105	11,025	100	10,000	10,500
4	115	13,225	102	10,404	11,730
5	117	13,689	118	13,924	13,806
6	106	11,236	105	11,025	11,130
7	102	10,404	100	10,000	10,200
8	100	10,000	100	10,000	10,000
9	98	9604	85	7225	8330
10	113	12,769	119	14,161	13,447

$N = 10$ $\Sigma X = 1071$ $\Sigma X^2 = 115,377$ $\Sigma Y = 1044$ $\Sigma Y^2 = 109,964$ $\Sigma XY = 112,443$

$\bar{X} = \Sigma X/N = 107.1$ $\bar{Y} = \Sigma Y/N = 104.4$

$$s_x = \sqrt{\Sigma X^2/(N - \overline{X}^2)}$$
$$= \sqrt{115,377/(10 - 107.1^2)}$$
$$= \sqrt{11,537.7 - 11,470.41}$$
$$= \sqrt{67.29}$$
$$= 8.20$$

Similarly,

$$s_y = \sqrt{\Sigma Y^2/(N - \overline{Y}^2)}$$
$$= \sqrt{109,964/(10 - 104.4^2)}$$
$$= \sqrt{10,996.4 - 10,899.36}$$
$$= \sqrt{97.04}$$
$$= 9.85$$
$$s_x s_y = 80.77$$

We can now complete our calculation of r by turning to the remainder of the formula:

$$r = \frac{\Sigma XY/(N - \overline{X}\,\overline{Y})}{80.77}$$

$$= \frac{112,443/[10 - (107.1) \times (104.4)]}{80.77}$$

$$= \frac{11,244.3 - 11,181.24}{80.77}$$

$$= \frac{63.06}{80.77}$$

$$= .781$$

The r of .78 indicates a strong, but not perfect, relationship between the two IQ scores. In the case of a perfect relationship, or a correlation of 1.00, all three variability estimates making up the correlational formula will be equal, and the following will be true:

$$s_x^2 = s_y^2 = \text{cov}_{xy}$$

where cov_{xy} is the covariance of the X and Y scores. Assume, for example, that $s_x^2 = s_y^2 = \text{cov}_{xy} = 1.00$ in the case of data yielding a perfect correlation. Now

$$r = \frac{100}{(\sqrt{100})(\sqrt{100})}$$

$$= \frac{100}{100}$$

$$= 1$$

If, on the other hand, we observe a perfect negative correlation (-1.00), the sum of the cross-products divided by $N[(\Sigma XY)/N]$ will always be smaller than the product of the X and Y means $(\overline{X}\overline{Y})$ by an amount equal to $s_x s_y$.

STATISTICAL INFERENCE

In the preceding section we discussed a number of statistical indexes that enable the researcher to evaluate the data from a behavioral study. We saw, for example, that such descriptive statistics as the mean, median, and mode can be used to summarize the central tendency of a distribution of scores. Similarly, the range, variance, and standard deviation provide a convenient way to describe the spread of variability of scores in a particular distribution.

Although these descriptive statistics can accurately and adequately summarize or describe a particular sample of observations, this is ordinarily not sufficient for the behavioral researcher. His real interest is not in knowing the exact characteristics of his sample but in determining, from his sample data, the characteristics of the population from which the sample was selected. The primary purpose of behavioral research lies in inferring population characteristics from sample statistics, or generalizing experimental results beyond those individuals who were included in a particular study. It is at this point in the research process that inferential statistics become extremely important to the behavioral scientist. In this section we will discuss the role of inferential statistics in estimating population characteristics from sample data, and then we will extend the discussion of statistical inference to the problem of testing scientific hypotheses about behavioral processes.

Parameters and Population Distributions

Applying inferential statistics to behavioral data enables us to estimate important characteristics of the population. For this purpose we can use the sample statistics, such as the mean $(\overline{X})$ and the standard deviation (s), to estimate the corresponding characteristics, or *parameters*, of the population.   To distinguish between statistics, which are computed from samples, and parameters, the true population values, it is customary to use Greek letters to represent parameters and Roman letters to represent statistics. Thus, $\bar{X}$ is used to represent the mean of a sample, while the Greek letter μ (mu) refers to the mean of the population. Similarly, s refers to a sample standard deviation, while σ (sigma) represents the standard deviation of a population.

To use statistics to estimate parameter values, the researcher must frequently make some assumptions about the way in which scores on his performance measure are distributed in the population. Ordinarily he will assume that the population distribution is approximately like the *normal distribution*. The normal distribution is a theoretical probability distribution that serves as the basis for a great many of the methods of inferential statistics. An example of a normal distribution is shown in Figure A.1.

In a normal distribution the mean, median, and mode are all equal, and these measures of central tendency define the highest point of the distribution. This distribution is also symmetrical in shape, with the frequency of scores the largest in the center, at the mean, and falling off at an equal rate on either side of the mean. A particular normal distribution is completely specified by two parameters—the mean and the standard deviation. The mean indicates the midpoint of the distribution, while the standard deviation reflects the spread of the scores on either side of the mean. Approximately 68 percent of the scores will fall within plus and minus one standard deviation unit of the mean in a normally distributed

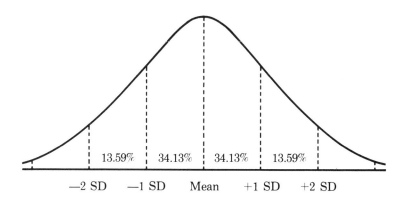

FIGURE A.1.   The normal distribution, showing the percentage of scores falling plus or minus one and two standard deviation units from the mean.

population, while the areas of the distribution between plus one to plus two standard deviation units and between minus one to minus two standard deviation units from the mean will each contain approximately 13.6 percent of the scores. A normally distributed population is assumed for a number of reasons. First, many natural events and measures are approximately normally distributed. Measures such as height, for example, tend to assume a normal distribution in nature. Many other behavioral measures are also known to be normally distributed in the population. A second important reason is that the statistical techniques designed to accomplish various types of statistical inference are most conveniently calculated if we assume a normal distribution. Although this might seem to be a relatively nonscientific reason for assuming a normal distribution for our population, theoretical statisticians have demonstrated a very important theorem that allows the researcher to use techniques based on the normal distribution even if the actual population is not normally distributed.

The central limit theorem states,

> If a population has a finite variance σ^2 and mean μ, then the distribution of sample means from samples of N independent observations approaches a normal distribution with variance σ^2/N and mean μ as sample size N increases. When N is very large, the sampling distribution of M [mean, or $\bar{X}$] is approximately normal [Hays, 1963, p. 238].

This theorem means that if we were to take a number of independent samples from a given population and compute a mean for each sample, a distribution made up of these sample means would assume the shape of a normal distribution even if the population from which the samples were drawn is not normal. Further, the principal characteristic of our samples that influences the normality of our distribution of the sample means is the sample size N. Thus, for large samples in particular, we can assume a normal distribution of sample means no matter what type of distribution characterizes our population. This fact allows us to use a number of statistical procedures that refer back to the normal distribution.

Estimating Population Parameters

Point Estimates.   In the estimation of true population values, or parameters, the researcher can state his estimates in one of two ways. On the one hand, he can take the sample statistics, after appropriate adjustments to correct biases due to sampling errors, as *point* estimates of the population parameters. In following this course of action, the researcher simply estimates the values of μ and σ, for example.

The sample mean, $\bar{X}$, is an unbiased estimate of the population parameter μ, and the expected value or best estimate of μ is, in fact, $\bar{X}$. The standard deviation, s, however, is not an unbiased estimate of σ; and s must be corrected for bias to provide our best estimate of the population standard deviation. The standard deviation computed from a sample will always underestimate σ by virtue of the sampling process itself. If we assume that the population from which we are sampling is normally distributed, we will find when we draw our sample of size N that scores near the center of the distribution will have a much greater chance of being included in the sample than scores at the extreme ends of the distribution. (Remember that 68 percent of the scores in a normal distribution are located within plus or minus one standard deviation unit from the mean.) As a consequence, the spread, or variability, of the scores of our sample distribution will be much smaller than the spread of scores in the population distribution; and our index of variability, s, will be too small to be an accurate estimate of the population. To correct for this bias present in s, we can use the following and thus provide an unbiased estimate of σ:

$$\hat{s} = \sqrt{\frac{N(s^2)}{N-1}}$$

Interval Estimation.   Although point estimates of population parameters provide the researcher's best single guess about the true characteristics of the population, it is frequently advantageous to estimate parameters such as μ by means of an inferential technique known as *interval* estimation. This procedure allows the experimenter to state a range of scores within which he can be sure, at some specified probability level, that the true parameter value will fall. The investigator, on the basis of these statistical techniques, can report, for example, that he is 95 percent confident that the actual value of μ, the population mean, will be within five points on either side of his sample mean $\bar{X}$.

As a first step in the determination of confidence intervals for the mean, it is necessary to calculate an index called the standard error of the mean (est $\sigma_{\bar{X}}$), which provides an estimate of the magnitude of the sampling error involved in the selection of a particular sample from the population. The sampling error of the mean is

$$\text{est } \sigma_{\bar{X}} = \frac{\hat{s}}{\sqrt{N}}$$

Notice that in the computation of this statistic we are using $\hat{s}$, our unbiased estimate of σ.

The standard error of the mean is based on the concept of a sampling distribution of means, which we discussed earlier. Essentially, est $\sigma_{\bar{X}}$ reflects the estimated standard deviation of this distribution of the means of all possible samples of size N drawn from the population. In this instance we are estimating the standard deviation of this theoretical distribution of sample means from the statistic $\hat{s}$, computed from a single sample of size N. The magnitude of est σ, or the sampling error, is greatly influenced by the sample size, N. As N becomes larger, the size of the standard error of the mean becomes smaller and, as we shall see shortly, the confidence interval for the mean becomes narrower.

In calculating the actual confidence interval for the mean, we will need, in addition to $\bar{X}$ and our est $\sigma_{\bar{X}}$, a coefficient obtained from tables of the normal distribution. This coefficient is called the z score and is associated with the confidence level we select for our interval estimate. If, for example, we wish to establish a confidence interval such that we can be 95 percent confident that the true mean, μ, is contained within the range, the z score associated with the probability of .95 is 1.96. We might then express our confidence interval for the mean as follows:

$$\bar{X} - 1.96 \text{ est } \sigma_{\bar{X}} \leq \mu \leq \bar{X} + 1.96 \text{ est } \sigma_{\bar{X}} \text{ for } p = .95$$

This expression indicates that we can be 95 percent confident that μ lies within the range of $\bar{X} \pm 1.96$ est $\sigma_{\bar{X}}$.

Tests of Hypotheses

In Chapter 6 we discussed, on at least a conceptual level, the second major area of inferential statistics: hypothesis testing. Recall that the procedures for the evaluation of hypotheses are designed to provide the researcher with grounds, in the form of specific test statistics, for making a choice between the alternative hypothesis and the null hypothesis, or hypothesis of no effect. In this section we will amplify the discussion of the hypothesis-testing procedures presented in Chapter 6 and provide additional computational detail to illustrate the application of each of the statistical techniques discussed.

The χ^2 Single Sample Test. As we indicated in our earlier discussion of hypothesis-testing procedures, the χ^2 single sample test is a nonparametric statistical procedure particularly suited to studies in which the dependent variable can be measured only on the nominal scale. To illustrate the computational steps involved in this hypothesis-testing procedure, we will use the data reported in Table 6.2 for the hypothetical study giving rise to the following alternative and null hypotheses:

H_1:   The number of drunk drivers on the road is not uniformly distributed as a function of time of day.

H_0:   The number of drunk drivers is uniformly distributed across time periods.

The data on which the χ^2 single sample test will be based are shown in Table A.8. The column headed k_i in this table contains the nominal scale label for the categories, or time periods; column O_i lists the number of drunks observed during each time period (from column 2 of Table 6.2); and column E_i shows the expected numbers for each time period if the null hypothesis were true. In our example each of the entries in column E_i is 33, since a total of 99 drunks was identified (see Table 6.2). If the null hypothesis were true and the same number of drunks were observed during each of the three time periods, there would be 99/3, or 33, drunks in each time period.

The statistical test of the null hypothesis is given by the following expression:

$$\chi^2 = \sum_{i=1}^{k} \frac{(O_i - E_i)^2}{E_i}$$

where χ^2 = the statistical index computed by the test

O_i = the observed frequency for the ith category

E_i = the expected frequency for the ith category provided that H_0 is true

$\sum_{i=1}^{k}$ = summing the quantity $(O - E)^2/E$ over all k categories

TABLE A.8.   Hypothetical data for χ^2 single sample test: observed and expected frequencies of drunk drivers by time period. There are three time period categories (k).

Time Period	k_i	O_i	E_i	$(O_i - E_i)^2/E_i$
7 PM-10 PM	1	13	33	12.12
10 PM-1 AM	2	33	33	0
1 AM-4 AM	3	53	33	12.12

$$\chi^2 = \sum_{i=1}^{k} \frac{(O_i - E_i)^2}{E_i} = 12.12 + 0 + 12.12 = 24.24$$

The χ^2 test whose formula is given above allows us to compare statistically the frequency distribution of expected values with the distribution of observed frequencies obtained from our sample. To the extent that the null hypothesis is true, the quantity $(O - E)^2/E$ (or the squared difference between observed and expected frequencies divided by the expected frequency) will be small for each time period, and the difference between O and E at each time period will reflect just a chance variation. On the other hand, if the alternative hypothesis is true and the null hypothesis false, each of these quantities $[(O - E)^2/E]$ will be relatively larger. Essentially, then, the more divergent, or different, the two frequency distributions (observed and expected), the larger the χ^2 value.

The statistical decision of whether to reject the null hypothesis involves, first, the selection of a significance level for the χ^2 test. Once again, the significance level (α) represents the probability of a Type I error. As we have indicated, a conventional level of α used in the behavioral sciences is the .05 level, which holds the probability of a Type I error to 5 percent. It should be emphasized at this point that α should be established prior to the computation of the χ^2 rather than as a matter of convenience after the analysis is complete.

Equipped with a given α value, the χ^2, and another index, degrees of freedom (df), we can then consult a table of the χ^2 distribution to determine whether to reject the null hypothesis in favor of the alternative hypothesis. The degrees of freedom (df) are simply $k - 1$, where k is the number of categories (time periods in this case). In our example, $\alpha = .05$, $\chi^2 = 24.24$, and $df = 2$, since there are three time periods. Consulting a table of the χ^2 distribution, we find that the numeric value associated with two degrees of freedom and an α of .05 is 5.99. This figure indicates that we must obtain a χ^2 value of at least 5.99 to reject the null hypothesis in favor of its alternative. In our example the obtained χ^2 of 24.24 is well beyond this value, and we infer that the alternative hypothesis is correct.

The Sign Test.   In our discussion of the sign test in Chapter 6, we saw that this procedure is a nonparametric technique suited to studies that use pairs of subjects or studies that test the same subjects under different experimental conditions. Our example in Chapter 6 involved a comparison of husbands' and wives' attitudes toward women's liberation, and the data for the sign test consisted of a list of plus or minus signs resulting from the comparison of the husband's with the wife's attitude for each couple. A minus sign indicated that the wife's attitude was more favorable toward women's lib, while a plus sign indicated that the husband had the more positive attitude. A zero was recorded if both shared the same attitude. In this example we found two plus signs, six minus signs, and two zeros. The alternative hypothesis for this example stated:

H_1:   Husbands have a less positive attitude toward the women's libera- tion movement than do their wives.

The null hypothesis for this application of the sign test can be stated in a slightly more refined form:

$$H_0: p(X_h > X_w) = p(X_h < X_w) = \frac{1}{2}$$

where $p(X_h > X_w)$ indicates the probability (p) of the husbands' scores (X_h) being higher than the wives' scores (X_w) and $p(X_h < X_w)$ indicates the probability of X_h being lower than X_w.

The null hypothesis then states that the probability of a plus or a minus sign is equal and, since there are only two alternatives, that either probability is ½. On the basis of the null hypothesis, we would expect an equal number of pluses and minuses in our sample, and this is the basis for the sign test. The statistical decision of whether to reject the null hypothesis involves recording the number of fewer signs (two pluses in this case) and N (the number of pairs with a nonzero sign) and consulting a table of the binomial distribution. Since there are two zeros recorded in our example, these pairs are excluded from the analysis, and the N is reduced to eight pairs. The binomial distribution table will list the probabilities of obtaining the particular number of fewer signs (two pluses) out of N (eight) comparisons if the null hypothesis, stating pluses and minuses are equally likely, is true. In this instance the probability of obtaining as few as two pluses in eight observations is given as .145. If, as is conventional, we had established the .05 level as α for our test, we would be forced to decide not to reject the null hypothesis, since the binomial probability obtained was not equal to or less than .05.

Since the statistical hypothesis of our study predicted not only that the relative number of pluses and minuses would differ but also that there would be more pluses than minuses, our statistical test was *one-tailed*. In this case, as in most statistical tests, a one-tailed test evaluates both magnitude and direction of differences. A *two-tailed* test, on the other hand, evaluates only the magnitude, not the direction, of differences. A two-tailed sign test would have been appropriate if our prediction, on the basis of the statistical hypothesis, had been simply that the frequencies of pluses and minuses were different and not that one or the other sign would occur more frequently. The probability of our result (two plus signs in eight observations) would be a .29 for a two-tailed test, or twice as large as for the one-tailed test.

The Mann-Whitney U Test.   In Chapter 6 we discussed an application of the Mann-Whitney U Test as a nonparametric procedure for comparing the performance of independent groups of subjects. The computational steps discussed for this small-sample case in Chapter 6 need no amplification here, since the computation of the U statistic for small samples is a simple process of counting. The computational steps discussed in Chapter 6 are, however, restricted to studies in which the larger of the two groups compared consists of less than 20 subjects. Frequently, however, the researcher is faced with a situation in which his group sizes exceed this limit, so he must compute the U statistic in a slightly different manner. In this section we will illustrate the computational steps for the Mann-Whitney U Test for large samples. It should be noted, however, that the ultimate results of the two computational procedures are equivalent.

To illustrate the large-sample computation of the U test, let us assume that an investigator wished to determine whether noise is more annoying to individuals who are typically exposed to a noisy environment than to subjects who work in quiet places. His alternative hypothesis states:

> H_1:   Workers subjected to elevated noise levels in their work environment will show less annoyance upon exposure to intense noise than will workers whose work environments are relatively quiet.

To test this hypothesis, the researcher selected one group of 15 subjects from among the employees of a local steel mill and another group of 21 subjects from among the attendants employed by a rural rest home. The subjects in both groups were brought into the investigator's laboratory, subjected for five minutes to 100 decibels of noise, and then asked to rate the annoyance level produced by this noise on a 25-point rating scale. The annoyance score for each subject could therefore range from 1 to 25, with 1 being the least and 25 the most annoying. The data for this hypothetical study are presented in Table A.9.

In the calculation of the Mann-Whitney U statistic for this large-sample case, we will use slightly different procedures than for the small-sample case discussed in Chapter 6. Once again, however, the actual statistical evaluation of the data is based on the composite ranking of scores from both groups. The second and fourth columns list the ranks of each individual in both groups in annoyance score magnitude. Note

TABLE A.9.   Hypothetical data for a large-sample Mann-Whitney U Test comparing the noise annoyance ratings of two groups.

	Group 1			Group 2	
	Score	Rank		Score	Rank
1	15	19.5	1	17	25.5
2	17	24.5	2	19	28.5
3	20	30	3	15	19.5
4	8	7.5	4	9	10
5	14	16.5	5	12	13.5
6	9	10	6	13	15
7	7	5.5	7	15	19.5
8	12	13.5	8	21	31
9	5	3	9	24	34
10	6	4	10	25	35.5
11	4	2	11	22	32.5
12	10	12	12	18	27
13	9	10	13	17	24.5
14	7	5.5	14	16	22
15	2	1	15	15	19.5
			16	14	16.5
			17	19	28.5
			18	22	32.5
			19	17	24.5
			20	8	7.5
			21	25	35.5
		$R_1 = 164.5$			$R_2 = 502.5$

that there are several tied ranks in this composite set of data. The procedure for handling ties is to assign each of the tied scores the mean of the tied ranks. The first tie in our example involves the score of 7, obtained by subjects 7 and 14 in group 1. Both of these individuals are assigned the rank of 5.5 because the two ranks involved are 5 and 6 and two individuals are tied for them; hence $(5 + 6)/2 = 5.5$.

Since the procedure for obtaining the values of U and U' with the procedure used for the small-sample case would be very cumbersome with such large samples, we use the following formula:

$$U = n_1 n_2 + \frac{n_1(n_1 + 1)}{2} - R_1$$

and

$$U = n_1 n_2 + \frac{n_2(n_2 + 1)}{2} - R_2$$

where R_1 is the sum of the ranks assigned to the individuals in group 1 and R_2 is the sum of the ranks assigned in group 2. For our example the two U values are

$$U = n_1 n_2 + \frac{n_2(n_2 + 1)}{2} - R_2$$

$$= (15)(21) + \frac{(21)(22)}{2} - 502.5$$

$$= 315 + 231 - 502.5$$

$$= 43.5$$

and

$$U' = n_1 n_2 + \frac{n_1(n_1 + 1)}{2} - R_1$$

$$= (15)(21) + (15)(16) - 164.5$$

$$= 315 + 120 - 164.5$$

$$= 270.5$$

These formulas yield results exactly equivalent to the procedure used with the small-sample case but provide a welcome shortcut when we deal with larger samples.

To determine the significance of the U of 43.5 obtained in this hypothetical study, we must first convert the U statistic to a z score by the following formula:

$$z = \frac{U - (n_1 n_2/2)}{\sqrt{[n_1 n_2 (n_1 + n_2 + 1)]/12}}$$

or for our example:

$$z = \frac{43.5 - [(15)(21)]/2}{\sqrt{[(15)(21)(15 + 21 + 1)]/12}}$$

$$= \frac{43.5 - 157.5}{\sqrt{971.25}}$$

$$= 3.66$$

Consulting a table of the normal distribution, we find that the probability of obtaining a z score this extreme is approximately .0001. We can therefore be quite confident in rejecting the null hypothesis, which held that the annoyance ratings of the two groups were drawn from the same population.

The t Test for Independent Samples.   The t test for two independent samples is the parametric equivalent of the Mann-Whitney U Test and, as a parametric statistical procedure, requires that the measures of behavior in studies to which it is applied be taken on at least the interval scale of measurement. In Chapter 6 we introduced the t test at only a conceptual level, and we suggested alternative and null hypotheses that might be appropriately tested with this form of the t test. These hypotheses are as follows:

H₁: Children from higher socioeconomic class families show higher mean intelligence, as measured by IQ test X, than children of low socioeconomic class families.

H₀: The mean IQs of the populations of high socioeconomic class and low socioeconomic class children are equal.

To test H₁ against H₀, we might randomly select two groups of ten children each and administer IQ test X, which we assume provides at least an interval scale measurement of intelligence. One group will be selected from high socioeconomic class children, the other from a population of low socioeconomic class children. The data for this hypothetical study are shown in Table A.10.

TABLE A.10.   Hypothetical data for the t test for independent samples.

Low Socioeconomic Class		High Socioeconomic Class	
Subject	IQ Score (X_1)	Subject	IQ Score (X_2)
1	90	1	125
2	100	2	120
3	105	3	105
4	125	4	90
5	100	5	75
6	115	6	100
7	95	7	130
8	105	8	115
9	110	9	100
10	85	10	105

$$\Sigma X_1 = 1030 \qquad \Sigma X_2 = 1065$$
$$\overline{X}_1 = 103 \qquad \overline{X}_2 = 106.5$$
$$s_1^2 = 126 \qquad s_2^2 = 250.25$$
$$\hat{s}_1^2 = 139.99 \qquad \hat{s}_2^2 = 278.03$$
$$n_1 = 10 \qquad n_2 = 10$$

As a first step in the calculation of the test statistic t, which provides the test of the null hypothesis against the alternative hypothesis, we must statistically describe each sample by computing means, variances, and standard deviations. We find that the mean IQ for the low socioeconomic group is 103 and s_1^2 is 126. Applying the correction to remove the bias in s_1^2, we find that:

$$\hat{s}_1^2 = \frac{n_1}{n_1 - 1}(s_1^2) = \left(\frac{10}{9}\right)(126) = 139.99$$

and therefore

$$\hat{s}_1 = \sqrt{\hat{s}_1^2} = 11.83$$

Similarly, for the high socioeconomic group, we find that $\overline{X}_2 = 106.5$, $s_2^2 = 250.25$, and $\hat{s}_2^2 = (10/9)(250.25) = 278.03$, with $\hat{s}_2 = \sqrt{278.03} = 16.67$. We can then estimate the standard error of the mean for each sample as follows:

$$\text{est } \sigma_m = \frac{\hat{s}}{\sqrt{n}}$$

For group 1:

$$\text{est } \sigma_{m1} = \frac{11.83}{\sqrt{n_1}} = \frac{11.83}{\sqrt{10}} = 3.74$$

For group 2:

$$\text{est } \sigma_{m2} = \frac{16.67}{\sqrt{n_2}} = \frac{16.67}{\sqrt{10}} = 5.27$$

We can now use these statistics to compute the value of the test statistic t, which we will use in our decision of whether to reject H_0.

$$t = \frac{\overline{X}_1 - \overline{X}_2}{\text{est } \sigma_{\text{diff}}}$$

where est σ_{diff}, or the estimated standard error of the difference, is given by:

$$\text{est } \sigma_{\text{diff}} = \sqrt{\text{est } \sigma_{\overline{X}_1}^2 + \text{est } \sigma_{\overline{X}_2}^2}$$

or for our example,

$$\text{est } \sigma_{\text{diff}} = \sqrt{139.99 + 278.03} = 20.44$$

Completing the calculation of t, we then have

$$t = \frac{103 - 106.5}{20.44} = -.171$$

Once again, we will consult a statistical table to determine whether the value of the test statistic (t) obtained is large enough to indicate rejection of the null hypothesis. We will use a significance level (α) of .05 and the degrees of freedom for the t test to determine the critical value of t that will allow us to reject the null hypothesis. Degrees of freedom in this case are given by:

$$df = (n_1 - 1) + (n_2 - 1) = (10 - 1) + (10 - 1) = 18$$

The critical value of t for an α of .05 and 18 degrees of freedom is 1.734, indicating that if we are to reject the null hypothesis we must obtain a t this large or larger. On the basis of the obtained result ($t = .171$), we cannot reject the null hypothesis and must conclude that there is no difference in the mean IQ between high and low socioeconomic class children.

The version of the t test that we have used in the example requires that independent samples of size n_1 and n_2 be used, and it is not appropriate for cases in which we have obtained our performance measure by testing the same group of subjects on two separate occasions or under two different treatment conditions. The purpose of this t test is to determine whether the contention of the null hypothesis that the two independent samples have been drawn from the same population is tenable.

The t Test for Correlated Observations

Behavioral scientists frequently encounter research situations in which they wish to test hypotheses about the performance of a single group of subjects tested under two different conditions or hypotheses about the assessment of differences in behavior between correlated pairs of individuals or observations. An example of the latter case was used in our discussion of the sign test, in which husband and wife pairs were compared. The t test for correlated observations provides the parametric equivalent of the sign test but uses the increased information available in interval or ratio scale measurement.

To illustrate this version of the parametric t test, let us consider the following alternative hypothesis:

H$_1$:   The mean reaction time of individuals at a BAC of .10 percent is greater than that under conditions of 0 percent BAC.

This hypothesis leads us to the null hypothesis:

H$_0$:   The mean reaction times of humans are not different at BAC levels of .10 percent and 0 percent.

As in our previous use of H$_0$, the null hypothesis states that the treatment condition will produce no effect on reaction time performance. In contrast to the t test for two independent samples, the t test for correlated observations will treat the data as though we had a single sample of n pairs of measures rather than two separate samples of n_1 and n_2 observations. The data for this example might take the form shown in Table A.11, which shows the reaction time measure taken for each of ten hypothetical

TABLE A.11.   Hypothetical data for the t test for correlated observations.

| Subject | Choice Reaction Time Score | | D_i | D_i^2 |
	Alcohol	No Alcohol		
1	1.45	1.05	+.40	.16
2	1.75	1.00	+.75	.562
3	.95	.95	0	0
4	2.05	1.50	+.55	.302
5	2.15	2.00	+.15	.022
6	.95	1.00	−.05	.002
7	1.65	1.75	−.10	.010
8	2.10	1.40	+.70	.490
9	2.50	1.60	+.90	.810
10	1.45	1.00	+.45	.202

$N = 10$ $\qquad\qquad\qquad\qquad\qquad\qquad\qquad\qquad$ $\Sigma D_i = 3.75 \qquad \Sigma D_i^2 = 2.56$

$$M_D = \frac{\Sigma D_i}{N} = .375 \qquad s_D^2 = \frac{\Sigma D_i^2}{N} - M_D^2 = .115$$

$$\text{est } \sigma_{MD} = \frac{s_D}{\sqrt{N-1}} = \frac{.339}{3} = .113$$

$$t = \frac{M_D}{\text{est } \sigma_{MD}} = 3.32$$

subjects under each condition. Now, instead of computing statistical indexes for two separate samples, we will concentrate on the differences between reaction time scores under the two treatment conditions. The column headed D_i in Table A.11 shows the difference between each subject's reaction time score under the control, or zero percent BAC, condition and the treatment, or .10 percent BAC, condition.

To calculate the t statistics for correlated observations from these difference scores, a somewhat different set of procedures will be used. First, we must compute the mean of the difference scores—M_D, or the average difference observed between treatment and control conditions.

$$M_D = \frac{\Sigma D_i}{N} = \frac{3.75}{10} = .375$$

Thus, on the average, the reaction times under the alcohol condition were .375 seconds slower than in the no alcohol condition. Next, we can calculate the variance of the deviations (s_D^2) as follows:

$$s_D^2 = \frac{\Sigma D_i^2}{N} - M_D^2 = \frac{.256}{10} - .141 = .115$$

This variability measure then allows us to calculate an estimate of the standard error of the mean difference by:

$$\text{est } \sigma_{MD} = \frac{s_D}{\sqrt{N-1}} = \frac{.339}{3} = .113$$

Finally, we can compute the t statistic for correlated observations as follows:

$$t = \frac{M_D}{\text{est } \sigma_{MD}} = \frac{.375}{.113} = 3.32$$

We must again determine the significance level for the test by consulting a table of the t distribution to determine the critical value of t required to reject the null hypothesis at that level of α and for the appropriate degrees of freedom. Degrees of freedom in this case are given as $N - 1$, or one less than the number of pairs of observations; therefore, $df = 9$. The critical value of t for an α of .05 and a df of 9 is 2.262. Since the t of 3.32 obtained in our study exceeds this critical value, we can reject the null hypothesis in favor of our alternative hypothesis, which predicts a difference in reaction time between the control and treatment conditions. Again, the α level of .05 assures us that the probability of a Type I error does not exceed 5 percent.

Analysis of Variance

To illustrate the computational procedures involved in the analysis of variance, we will consider the example suggested in Chapter 6 that involved a hypothetical study comparing the IQ scores of children from three socioeconomic classes. For computational simplicity we might administer the IQ test to three groups of five children each to determine whether there are differences in IQ as a function of socioeconomic status. Table A.12 contains the hypothetical data for this example.

For each of the three groups, we can sum the five IQ scores and calculate three separate sums and three separate means, as shown in the table. We can also compute a grand total (G) and a grand mean $(\bar{G})$, which are the sum and the mean of all 15 IQ scores. Each group mean $(\bar{X}_1, \bar{X}_2,$ and $\bar{X}_3)$ defines the center of its distribution of IQ scores, and the individual scores within each set of five are spread out, or vary, around their particular means. Similarly, the grand mean $(\bar{G})$ defines the center of the entire distribution of scores from all three groups; and these scores vary around $\bar{G}$.

It is also true, however, that $\bar{G}$ also defines the center of another distribution of scores, consisting of the three group means, and that $\bar{X}_1,$ $\bar{X}_2,$ and $\bar{X}_3$ vary around G. We can see, then, that we have two distinct kinds of variability, or variance, associated with our set of data. On the one hand, we have the variance associated with the spread of individual scores around their respective group means, and, on the other, we have variance associated with the spread of the group means around the grand mean. As the name of the technique suggests, the purpose of the analysis of variance is to discriminate between these different kinds of variability.

TABLE A.12. Hypothetical data for simple one-way analysis of variance: IQ scores of low, middle, and high socioeconomic status children.

Low Status (X_1)	Middle Status (X_2)	High Status (X_3)
100	135	100
105	120	90
110	115	85
95	125	105
125	100	100
$\Sigma X_1 = 535$	$\Sigma X_2 = 595$	$\Sigma X_3 = 480$
$\bar{X}_1 = 107$	$\bar{X}_2 = 119$	$\bar{X}_3 = 96$

$$G = 1610 \qquad \bar{G} = 107.33$$

In our example the variability of the group means around the grand mean is interpreted to be the direct result of the independent variable, socioeconomic status. The variability of each score around its group mean, on the other hand, is considered to be error variance, or variability due to any factor besides the independent variable. In the analysis of variance, the total variance present in the data is simply the sum of variance due to group effects plus the error variance contributed by the differences in the IQ scores of the subjects in each group.

An index of variability used in the analysis of variance is called the sum of squared deviations (SS). The total variability of the data from the study is SS_{total}, which is given as follows:

$$SS_{total} = \Sigma\Sigma(X_{ij} - \overline{G})^2$$

The double summation notation ($\Sigma\Sigma$) indicates that the squared deviations $[(X_{ij} - \overline{G})^2]$ are to be added for each child ($i = 1\text{-}5$) at each economic level ($j = 1\text{-}3$). Thus, SS_{total} is the sum of the squared deviations of each of the 15 individual scores from the grand mean. The two components of this total variability, or sum of squares, are SS_{groups}, which can be defined as:

$$SS_{groups} = n(X_j - \overline{G})^2$$

or n times the sum of the squared deviations of each of the group means from the grand mean, and SS_{error}, which is

$$SS_{error} = (X_{ij} - X_j)^2$$

or the sum of the squared deviations of each individual score from its own group mean. For our example we find the following:

$$SS_{total} = (100 - 107.3)^2 + (105 - 107.3)^2 + (110 - 107.3)^2$$
$$+ \cdots (100 - 107.3)^2 = 2793.35$$

The portion of this total variation contributed by group effects is:

$$SS_{error} = (100 - 107)^2 + \cdots (125 - 107)^2 + (135 - 119)^2$$
$$+ \cdots (100 - 119)^2 + (100 - 96)^2 + \cdots (100 - 96)^2$$

We can check our computations by checking to see that

$$SS_{total} = SS_{groups} + SS_{error}$$

Thus,

$$2793.35 = 1323.35 + 1470$$

The various sums of squares we have calculated represent the total variability in the experiment due to their respective sources (that is, total versus group versus error variability). We can, however, calculate the average variability for each of the three sources. This average variation, or mean square (MS), is obtained by dividing each SS by its degrees of freedom and is the equivalent of the s^2 we have used in other statistical procedures. The degrees of freedom in each instance are given as the number of squared deviations entering into the calculation of the SS minus the number of points around which the deviations are calculated. Thus, in our calculation of the SS_{total}, we summed the deviations of the 15 scores (five per group) from the grand mean. The degrees of freedom associated with SS_{total} are, therefore, 15 squared deviations minus one grand mean, or 14. Similarly, in the calculation of SS_{groups}, we were concerned with the squared deviations of the three group means about the grand mean, so the degrees of freedom for this source are $3 - 1$, or 2. Finally, in computing the SS_{error}, we summed the squared deviations of each of the five scores in each group about the group mean. In this case we have $5 - 1$, or 4, degrees of freedom for group 1; 4 degrees of freedom for group 2; and 4 degrees of freedom for group 3. The degrees of freedom for SS_{error}, summing across all three groups, is therefore: $(5 - 1) + (5 - 1) + (5 - 1) = 12$. We can again check on the accuracy of our calculations of degrees of freedom by determining that:

$$df_{total} = df_{groups} + df_{error}$$

Having determined the appropriate degrees of freedom for each source of variation, we can now calculate the mean square, or average variability, of each source of variation:

$$MS_{total} = \frac{SS_{total}}{df_{total}} = \frac{2793.35}{14} = 199.53$$

$$MS_{groups} = \frac{SS_{groups}}{df_{groups}} = \frac{1323.35}{2} = 661.68$$

$$MS_{error} = \frac{SS_{error}}{df_{error}} = \frac{1470}{12} = 122.50$$

The actual statistical test used in the analysis of variance is the F ratio, which is calculated as the ratio of MS_{groups} to MS_{error}, or for our example:

$$F = \frac{MS_{groups}}{MS_{error}} = \frac{661.68}{122.50} = 5.40$$

To determine the significance of the F, we once again must consult a statistical table while armed with a predetermined α level and the degrees of freedom of both the numerator ($df_{groups} = 2$) and the denominator ($df_{error} = 12$) of the F ratio. We find that the critical F value at the .05 level for 2 and 12 degrees of freedom is 3.89. Since our F exceeds this value, we can reject the null hypothesis, which states that no differences due to socioeconomic group effects would be observed.

REFERENCES

American Psychological Association. *Publication manual*. Washington, D.C.: Author, 1967.

American Psychological Association. *Ethical principles in the conduct of research with human participants*. Washington, D.C.: Author, 1973.

Arnoult, M. D. *Fundamentals of scientific method in psychology*. Dubuque, Iowa: William C. Brown, 1972.

Berelson, B., & Steiner, G. *Human behavior*. New York: Harcourt, 1964.

Bitterman, E. M. Phyletic differences in learning. In J. M. Foley, R. A. Lockhart, & O. M. Messick (Eds.), *Contemporary readings in psychology*. New York: Harper, 1970.

Campbell, D. T., & Stanley, J. C. *Experimental and quasi-experimental designs for research*. Chicago: Rand McNally, 1966.

Chapanis, A. The relevance of laboratory studies to practical situations. *Ergonomics*, 1967, **10**, 557–577.

Guilford, J. P. *Psychometric methods*. (1st ed.) New York: McGraw-Hill, 1936.

Harlow, H. F., & Harlow, M. K. The affectional systems. In A. M. Schrier, H. F. Harlow, & F. Stollnitz (Eds.), *Behavior of nonhuman primates*. Vol. 2. New York: Academic Press, 1965.

Hays, W. L. *Statistics for psychologists*. New York: Holt, 1963.

Heimstra, N. W., & Ellingstad, V. *Human behavior: A systems approach*. Monterey, Calif.: Brooks/Cole, 1972.

Heimstra, N. W., Nichols, J., & Martin, G. An experimental methodology for analysis of child pedestrian behavior. *Pediatrics*, 1969, **44**(5, part 2), 832–838.

Kelman, H. C. Human use of human subjects: The problem of deception in social psychological experiments. *Psychological Bulletin*, 1967, **67**, 1–11.

Kerlinger, F. N. *Foundations of behavioral research*. New York: Holt, 1964.

Krathwohl, D. R. *How to prepare a research proposal*. Syracuse, N.Y.: Syracuse University Bookstore, 1966.

Olson, P., & Davis, J. H. Devisable tasks and pooling performance in groups. *Psychological Reports*, 1964, **15**, 511–517.

Rosenthal, R., & Rosnow, R. *Artifact in behavioral research*. New York: Academic Press, 1969.

Scott, W. A., & Wertheimer, M. *Introduction to psychological research*. New York: Wiley, 1962.

Selltiz, C., Jahoda, M., Deutsch, M., & Cook, S. *Research methods in social relations*. New York: Holt, 1962.

Sidowski, J. B., & Lockard, R. B. Some preliminary considerations in research. In J. B. Sidowski (Ed.), *Experimental methods and instrumentation in psychology*. New York: McGraw-Hill, 1966.

Siegel, S. *Nonparametric statistics for the behavioral sciences*. New York: McGraw-Hill, 1956.

Skinner, B. F. *Science and human behavior*. New York: Macmillan, 1953.

Suchman, E. A. *Evaluative research*. New York: Russell Sage Foundation, 1967.

Thompson, R., & McConnell, J. V. Classical conditioning in the planarian, *Dugesia dorotocephala*. *Journal of Comparative and Physiological Psychology*, 1955, **48**, 65–68.

Weick, K. E., Systematic observational methods. In G. Lindzey & E. Aronson (Eds.), *The handbook of social psychology*. (2nd ed.) Reading, Mass.: Addison-Wesley, 1968.

Wilson, E. B., Jr. *An introduction to scientific research*. New York: McGraw-Hill, 1952.

Winer, B. J. *Statistical principles in experimental design*. (2nd ed.) New York: McGraw-Hill, 1971.

INDEX

E